THE POWER OF
FAVOR

The Force That Will Take You
Where You Can't Go on Your Own

JOEL OSTEEN

New York   Nashville

ALSO BY JOEL OSTEEN

**All Things Are Working
for Your Good**

*Daily Readings from All Things Are
Working for Your Good*

Blessed in the Darkness

Blessed in the Darkness Journal

*Blessed in the Darkness
Study Guide*

Break Out!

Break Out! Journal

Daily Readings from Break Out!

Every Day a Friday

Every Day a Friday Journal

*Daily Readings from Every Day a
Friday*

Fresh Start

Fresh Start Study Guide

I Declare

*I Declare Personal Application
Guide*

Next Level Thinking

Next Level Thinking Journal
Next Level Thinking Study Guide
*Daily Readings from Next Level
Thinking*

The Power of Favor

The Power of Favor Study Guide

The Power of I Am

The Power of I Am Journal
The Power of I Am Study Guide
*Daily Readings from The Power
of I Am*

Think Better, Live Better

Think Better, Live Better Journal
Think Better, Live Better Study Guide
*Daily Readings from Think Better,
Live Better*

**Two Words That Will Change
Your Life Today**

With Victoria Osteen

Our Best Life Together
Wake Up to Hope Devotional

You Can, You Will

You Can, You Will Journal
*Daily Readings from You Can,
You Will*

Your Best Life Now

Your Best Life Begins Each Morning
Your Best Life Now for Moms
Your Best Life Now Journal
Your Best Life Now Study Guide
*Daily Readings from Your
Best Life Now*
*Scriptures and Meditations for Your
Best Life Now*
Starting Your Best Life Now

THE POWER OF
FAVOR

FaithWords
Hachette Book Group
1290 Avenue of the Americas, New York, NY 10104
faithwords.com
twitter.com/faithwords

First Edition: December 2019

FaithWords is a division of Hachette Book Group, Inc.
The FaithWords name and logo are trademarks of Hachette Book Group, Inc.

The publisher is not responsible for websites (or their content) that are not owned by the publisher.

The Hachette Speakers Bureau provides a wide range of authors for speaking events. To find out more, go to www.hachettespeakersbureau.com or call (866) 376-6591.

Scripture quotation noted from the *Amplified Bible.* Copyright © 2015 by The Lockman Foundation, La Habra, CA 90631. All rights reserved. For permission to quote information visit www.lockman.org.

Library of Congress Control Number: 2019948236

ISBN: 978-1-4555-3433-3 (hardcover), 978-1-4555-3436-4 (ebook), 978-1-5460-3728-6 (international trade), 978-1-5460-1770-7 (South Africa), 978-1-5460-3852-8 (large print), 978-1-5460-1777-6 (signed edition), 978-1-5460-1778-3 (special signed edition)

Printed in the United States of America

LSC-C

10 9 8 7 6 5 4 3 2 1

CONTENTS

THE POWER OF
FAVOR

CHAPTER ONE

The Power of Favor

What God has in your future you can't accomplish on your own. There are places He's going to take you that you can't get to by yourself. There will be obstacles that look too big, dreams that seem impossible. You're going to need assistance for where you're going. The good news is, God has put something on you that gives you an advantage, something that will open doors that you can't open, something that will make you stand out in the crowd. It's called "favor." Favor will cause good breaks to come to you. Favor will take you from the background to the foreground. Favor will give you preferential treatment, things you don't deserve. You weren't next in line, but you got the promotion. On paper it didn't make sense, but the loan went through. That person who was so against you—for some reason they've changed. Now they're for you. That wasn't a coincidence. That was the favor of God.

We can work hard, be faithful, be diligent, and that's important, but that will only take us to a certain level.

We'll go as far as our education, as far as our background allows. But when God breathes His favor on you, things will happen that you couldn't make happen; opportunities will open that you didn't see coming. The right people will track you down. I've heard it said, "One touch of favor is worth more than a lifetime of labor." Just one good break, one phone call, meeting one person can catapult you to a new level. You've worked hard. You've been faithful. You've honored God. Now get ready for favor. Get ready for God to show out. He's about to do something unusual, something that you haven't seen, good breaks that you didn't work for, a promotion that you didn't deserve. You can't explain it. You can't take credit for it. It's the favor of God.

God told Noah to build an ark, a 450-foot-long boat. Noah wasn't a builder. That wasn't his profession. It seemed impossible, but God will never ask you to do something and not give you the favor to do it. You have favor. The question is, Do you have the faith? Are you going to talk yourself out of it? "I don't have the resources. I don't know the right people. I don't have the talent." That's okay, because you have something that makes up for all of that: Favor is on your life.

It's good to have education, but education alone is not enough. Talent alone is not enough. You need favor for where you're going. You may not know the right people, but don't worry, God does. He has already lined up divine connections, people who will come into your life and use their influence to open doors, to give you opportunity that will push you forward. You don't have to manipulate people, try to convince them to like you, or compromise to get your way. If someone is not for you, you don't need them. Don't waste time trying to win them over. The people whom God has lined up for you don't have a choice. They may not like you, but they will help you anyway. They will go out of their way to be good to you. You don't have to find them. They will find you. You keep honoring God, believing

The favor on your life will cause the right people to show up.

and expecting. The favor on your life will cause the right people to show up.

The people in Noah's day didn't care anything about God. They were living wildly, partying, and worshipping idols. God was so upset that He was about to destroy the Earth through a great flood. He could have wiped everyone out and started over, but the Scripture says, "Noah found favor in the eyes of the Lord." Why did he find favor and not all the other people around him who were about to perish? The next verse says, "Noah continually followed God's will and did what was right." Noah could have compromised, fit in, done what everyone else was doing, but he made the choice to walk in obedience. When you honor God, when you keep Him first place, you will find favor in the eyes of the Lord. There is a blessing on your life that will push you up when others are going down.

Favor Brings You into Prominence

"Well, if I have favor, why am I having these difficulties? Why did these people come against me? Why did business slow down?" Having favor doesn't mean you won't have challenges, but favor is what's going to keep the challenges from defeating you, and sometimes God will put you in a situation so He can show you His favor. One definition of *favor* is "to endorse, to bring to prominence, to give notoriety." If you ask someone to endorse your book, you find a person who has more influence, more credibility, a bigger following than you. When they put their name on your book, their prominence instantly gives you more credibility.

Oprah Winfrey used to have her book club. When she would endorse a book, the author might have been unknown. Nobody had ever heard of them. Without the endorsement, the book would sell a few thousand copies. But when Oprah said on her talk show, "This is a great book. You should read it," that simple endorsement could cause the book to sell hundreds of thousands of copies.

It's great to have people's endorsement, but you need to get ready. The Creator of the universe is about to endorse you. God is going to make things happen that are so big, so amazing, that people will know it couldn't have been just

> *The Creator of the universe is about to endorse you.*

you. The medical report said you were done. "How'd you get well?" God endorsed you. His favor caused you to overcome what looked impossible. "How'd your business get so successful? How'd you get so far ahead? We went to the same school." God endorsed you. He showed His favor so people would know that you belong to Him.

This is what happened to Daniel in the Scripture. Favor didn't keep Daniel out of trouble. The trouble was a setup for God to endorse Daniel, to bring him into prominence. Daniel was a teenager living in a foreign country. The king made a decree that no one could pray to any god except to the king himself. But Daniel worshipped Jehovah. He made the decision that he wasn't going to compromise, so he kept praying just as he did every day. Some people saw him praying and ran and told the king. The king had Daniel thrown into a den of hungry lions. That should've been the end, but for some reason the lions couldn't open their mouths. I can hear one of those lions saying, "I'm hungry. I want to eat this guy, but my jaws are messed up."

Favor doesn't keep you out of the lions' den, but favor will keep the lions from harming you. The next morning the king went to check on Daniel. When he found out Daniel was okay, he said, "From now on we're all going to worship the God of Daniel."

"Well, Joel, maybe that was a lucky break. Maybe the lions weren't hungry that day." No, when they brought Daniel out of the lions' den, the king had them throw the people who were against Daniel into the den. Before they hit the bottom of the pit, the lions tore them apart. When people saw that, they knew the Lord was on Daniel's side.

God is going to do some things that bring you into prominence, into new levels of influence and credibility. People can debate what you say, but they can't debate what they see. When they see you running the company, paying your house off, and graduating with honors, they'll know God is endorsing you. When they see you breaking the addiction, beating the cancer, coming out of the lions' den unharmed, and accomplishing dreams way over your head, they will know God's hand is on your life and He's about to bring you into greater prominence. You've been in the background long enough, serving faithfully, helping others with no recognition. Your time is coming.

David spent years in the shepherds' fields taking care of his father's sheep, and I'm sure at times he thought, *I don't have favor. I'll never do anything great. I'm stuck out here. Nobody believes in me.* The truth is, you don't have to have people believe in you. The Most High God believes in you. When David defeated Goliath, that one good break, that one endorsement, launched him into a new level of his destiny, and it made up for all those lonely years. You may feel like you're falling behind, like it's too late to accomplish a dream, like you'll never get well. What God can do for you in one moment will put you fifty years down the road. That's the power of God endorsing you.

The Seal of Approval

You've seen a seal of approval on certain products. It may be stamped on the outside of a company's box, and it can be on a little-known product. Nobody's ever heard of it. But when that big company puts their stamp on it, their seal of approval, that product has notoriety and prominence, not because of what it is, but because of who endorsed it. The Creator of the universe is about to put His stamp on you. He's already accepted and approved you, but He's about to endorse you. He's about to go public. He's going to show people that you belong to Him. You're going to accomplish what you couldn't accomplish on your own. People are going to go out of their way to help you. You're going to defeat giants that are much bigger. People don't think you have a chance, but they don't know what's on you. They can't see the favor yet, but when God endorses you, when He shows out, they're not going to have any doubt that the Lord is on your side.

Joseph's brothers threw him into a pit and eventually sold him into slavery. He was falsely accused of a crime, put in prison for something he didn't do. All the odds were against him. But the Scripture says, "Joseph had favor in everything he did." One thing I've learned is that you can't keep a favored man down. You can't keep a favored woman down. You may have some obstacles, situations that are unfair. That doesn't mean you don't have favor. Challenges come to

> *Favor is why you're going to rise back to the top.*

us all, but favor is why you're not going to stay down. Favor is why you're going to rise back to the top.

Joseph spent thirteen years in the background, being overlooked and mistreated. There were plenty of lonely nights. He didn't get bitter. He kept doing the right thing. One day, Pharaoh had a dream that no one could interpret, so they brought Joseph out of prison and into Pharaoh's presence. Now he was standing in front of one of the most powerful people of that day. Joseph interpreted the dream. Pharaoh was so impressed that he made Joseph the prime minister, second in command. I can imagine that meeting took no longer than an hour. Joseph walked in as an imprisoned slave. An hour later, he walked out as the prime minister.

You don't know what God can do in an hour. He can take years of heartache, years of being overlooked, years of praying, believing, not seeing any good breaks, and in one hour He not only can deliver you, not only bring a dream to pass, but He can do something that catapults you to a new level of your destiny. How can this happen? The favor on your life. When God breathes on you, doors will open supernaturally. Obstacles that look permanent will turn around. People who were against you will suddenly be for you.

Years later, Joseph's brothers came to the palace looking for food—the same ones who had thrown him into the pit. There was a great famine in their country, and they had traveled to Egypt. Now Joseph, the prime minister, was in charge of the food supply. The brothers had done their best to keep him down, but God knows how to endorse you. He knows how to put you in a position of prominence.

You may feel like you're in a pit today. Don't get discouraged. We all have pit stops along the way in life. The good news is, that is not your final destination. God has an endorsement coming, and I've learned that the greater the opposition, the greater the endorsement. Much as with a bow and arrow, the more the enemy tries to pull you back, the more you're going to go forward. He thinks he's pulling you back to hinder you. He doesn't realize he's setting you up to shoot farther than you've ever imagined. When God says it's time, you're going to shoot into prominence, shoot into new levels of influence, leadership, respect, income, and credibility.

When the brothers saw Joseph and finally realized who he was, they nearly passed out. They thought they had gotten rid of him. But what they meant for harm, God used for good. God is not going to just deliver you, not going to just bring you out, He's going to endorse you. He's going to put you in a position of prominence where people can see you honored, respected, and admired.

You're Being Set Up for Endorsement

For over forty years, Lakewood Church was located in a neighborhood on the northeast side of Houston, and over time that area of the city became more industrial and a little more run-down. When I was growing up, Lakewood met in a small metal building, with metal folding chairs and a gravel parking lot. We had a portable wood building for the nurseries, and some people looked down on us because we couldn't afford much. We were second-class. We were at a disadvantage.

When I became pastor, there were certain people I saw during the week who weren't a part of Lakewood and wouldn't give me the time of day. They barely even acknowledged that I was there. But in December 2003, the Houston City Council voted for us to have the former Compaq Center as our building. We went from being in the industrial part of town with small roads, back in a neighborhood where hardly anybody could find us, to being on the second-busiest freeway in the nation in one of the most well-known, prestigious buildings in our city. That one good break catapulted us to levels of influence and respect that we couldn't have reached on our own in our whole lifetimes, and those same people who wouldn't give me the time of day started to ask me if I could save them seats. I told them, "Of course I will, right up by the flag."

What am I saying? God knows how to endorse you. He knows how to cause you to be seen in a different light. Don't be discouraged by where you are. God sees what's happening. He's keeping the records. He's going to make the wrongs right. He hears the disrespect. He hears them making fun. The Scripture says, "God heard Miriam criticizing Moses behind his back." They may not give you the time of day now, but don't worry, an endorsement is coming, not by people but by the Most High God.

> *He's going to do things that are out of your league, things you couldn't make happen.*

He's going to do things that are out of your league, things you couldn't make happen. He'll not only amaze you, but people around you are going to be amazed.

When people congratulated me for getting the Compaq Center, I thought, *If you only knew.* Yes, I prayed, and I believed, but God made things happen that I could never have made happen. The Scripture says, "God will turn the heart of a king." God turned council members who had been against us for years, and suddenly they were for us.

Right now, God is working behind the scenes in your life. He is setting you up for an endorsement, setting you up for something you've never seen—promotion, influence, relationships that will thrust you to a new level. That city council vote probably took ten minutes. The mayor brought the motion to the floor, there was a little discussion, and then they went around the table and fourteen council members voted. It's amazing what God can do in ten minutes. Those ten minutes changed the course of my life. It's amazing what God can do in an hour—Joseph meeting with the Pharaoh. It's amazing what God can do overnight—Daniel protected in the lions' den.

"That Day" for You Is Coming

God has some of these destiny moments already lined up for you. You can't see them now. If He showed you, you'd think, *There's no way.* But when God endorses you, it's not like when people show you favor. When God does it, it catapults you ahead, and it's not going to take a long time. Yes, you have to be faithful. Joseph was in difficult places for thirteen years, but it only took him an hour to get out. He didn't see it coming. He woke up that morning thinking it was another ordinary day in prison. He didn't know that was his day to be endorsed. He didn't know that day was a destiny moment.

What God has for you is going to happen unexpectedly. You're doing the right thing, honoring Him. Out of the blue, someone will call and offer you the promotion. The medical report will say no more cancer, the contract will go through, or you'll bump into the person of your dreams. What would happen

> *Father, thank You for endorsing me today.*

if we'd get up each day and say, "Father, thank You for endorsing me today. Let people see that I am Your child"?

As the Israelites were about to cross the Jordan River, God told Joshua, "Today I will begin to make you great in the eyes of all the Israelites." God was saying, "Joshua, this is your moment. I'm about to endorse you. People are going to see the greatness I've put in you. You've been in the background serving Moses, being faithful, but today you're coming into the foreground." Not long after that, Joshua led the Israelites into the Promised Land.

The Scripture says, "That day God made Joshua great in the eyes of all the people." God has a "that day" for you, a time when He will make you great, when He will cause you to stand out, where you will accomplish things you never dreamed you could accomplish. You will know it, and the people around you will see the greatness in you.

Helen Major was a longtime member of Lakewood. She taught elementary school for nearly forty years, faithfully pouring her best into the children. She got one promotion after another, then became assistant principal, then principal. After a very distinguished career, she retired. A few months later a new school was opening in the school district. The school board voted unanimously to name it the Helen Major Elementary School. She never dreamed a school would be named after her, but God knows how to endorse you. He knows how to make your life significant, and it's not so we can say, "Look who we are. Look how great we've become." It's about letting God's glory be seen through you. God wants to make you an example of His goodness, and if you will walk in humility and always give God the credit, there's no limit to how high He will take you.

Romans 8 says, "All creation is eagerly waiting for the day when God reveals who His children really are." That's talking about when we get to Heaven, but even now, God is going to show people that you belong to Him. All creation is waiting for you to come into *that day*. The stage has been set. The audience is in place. You keep honoring God, and He's going to show people who you really are. He's going to bring you into a position of greater prominence.

You may be behind the scenes as I used to be when I was doing the television production at Lakewood, and there's nothing wrong with that, but God has something bigger. He's going to use you to accomplish something significant, not just be a small part. You're going to shine. You're going to stand out. People are going to see the greatness in you. It's good to celebrate others. It's good to cheer your friends on. It's good to admire those who are ahead of you, but God doesn't want you to live in a cheerleader mode, always thinking about how great others are. Can I tell you that there is greatness in you? You have talent, creativity, ability, courage, and strength. It's going to come out in a greater way, and when you come into "that day" when God endorses you, people are going to step back and say, "Wow, I didn't know that was in them. I never dreamed they would shine that brightly." God is going to show people who you really are.

Favor Is Given to Fulfill Your Purpose

There was a young Jewish girl in the Scripture named Esther. She was an orphan, having lost both her parents. She was living in exile in Persia. It didn't look as though she would ever do anything great, but one day the king was looking for a new queen. He decided to have a nationwide beauty contest where he would choose the next queen. The king sent people out looking for young ladies, and they brought Esther back and put her in the contest. Esther had never been groomed to be a queen, never had the training. She didn't come from a prominent family. They lined all the young ladies up in front of the king. They were all beautiful, all wearing the latest fashions; all had the best hairdos and makeup. I can imagine the king looked at their résumés. Some of them came from wealth and influence. Some had impressive résumés, great educations, were standouts in their field. There were plenty of obvious choices, but for some reason the king chose Esther, an orphan, a foreigner.

When God endorses you, it will cause you to stand out. His favor will cause you to be preferred. They could've chosen anyone for the contract; for some reason they chose you. They could've bought any house in the neighborhood; for some reason they liked yours best. There were plenty of students who deserved the scholarship; for some reason they picked you. God knows how to make you attractive. He knows how to make people like you. Sometimes they don't even know why. They can't put their finger on it. There's just something about you. That's God smiling down on you.

"Well, Joel, this sounds good, but I don't have the training. I don't have the experience." Neither did Esther. Favor is more powerful than your résumé. Favor will take

> *Favor is more powerful than your résumé.*

you where you don't have the qualifications. Favor will open doors where you look up and think, *How did I get here? I was the least likely one.* Esther never dreamed of becoming a queen. That wasn't even on her radar. But when you come into "that day" when God endorses you, He will bring you into prominence that you've never imagined. He'll cause opportunity to come to you. Esther wasn't looking for that position. The position came to her. She went from the background to the foreground. Later, Esther used her position to save the Jewish people from a plot to destroy them. I believe one reason God gave her such prominence is that He knew she would use the influence to fulfill her purpose.

Favor is not about having a bigger house, a better car, or more stuff. There's nothing wrong with that, but that's not why God is going to favor you. Favor is given to fulfill your purpose. It's to advance His kingdom. When your dreams are tied to helping others, to making the world a better place, to lifting the fallen, then you will come into some of those "that day" moments when God will shine more on you than you've ever imagined. When God can trust you, He will take you from obscurity to notoriety.

Now you've worked hard, you've been faithful, you've honored God. Get ready, for the curtain is about to come up. God is about to show people who you really are. I believe and declare you are coming into a new level of prominence, a new level of influence, a new level of income. God is about to endorse you. People are going to see the greatness He put in you!

CHAPTER TWO

Declare Favor

One way our faith is released is through our words, and there is a connection between speaking favor and receiving favor. It's not enough to just believe you have favor. It's not enough to just expect favor. You have to take it one step further and declare favor. Every day you should declare, "I have the favor of God. Favor is on my family. Favor is on my health. Favor is on my business. Favor is on my finances." When you speak something out, you give it the right to come to pass. When you face difficult situations, instead of being discouraged, thinking, *Why did this happen?* you need to declare, "The favor of God is turning this around. Favor is bringing healing, freedom, vindication, and victory into my life."

It's one thing to think it, but when you declare it, angels go to work. In the unseen realm, things begin to change. We prayed, we believed, we hoped. That's good, but it's time to start speaking favor. Speak favor over your finances. "Father, thank You that Your favor is bringing me clients. Thank

You that Your favor is causing me to stand out. Thank You that what I touch will prosper and succeed." The Scripture says, "Jesus increased in favor with God and with people." You can increase in favor. The more you thank God for it, the more you declare it, the more favor you're going to see.

"Joel, you say I have favor, but I never get good breaks. I never see anything unusual." Maybe it's because you're not declaring it. Why don't you step it up a notch? All through the day say, "Father, thank You that Your favor is endorsing me. Thank You that Your favor is bringing me into prominence. Thank You that Your favor is taking me to new levels." That's not just being positive. That's releasing your faith for the favor of God.

Your Words Release Your Faith

There were five of us Osteen children growing up. We never left the house without my mother saying, "Father, thank You that my children have Your favor." I like to joke that it worked for all of us except my brother, Paul. Four out of five is not bad. But it's good to pray over your children. Ask God to protect them, guide them, give them wisdom, but don't stop there. Speak favor over them. "Father, thank You that my children have favor with their teachers, favor with other students, favor that causes them to excel."

David did this. He said, "Surely goodness and mercy will follow me all the days of my life." In one Bible translation, the word *goodness* is *favor*. David was saying, "Surely favor follows me all my life." In effect he was saying, "Favor is keeping enemies from defeating me. Favor is making me attractive. Favor is bringing promotion and opportunity." He didn't just think about it. He didn't just hope it would work out. He spoke favor over his life. No wonder the prophet Samuel came to him and anointed him the next king. No wonder he defeated a giant twice his size. No wonder King Saul couldn't kill him.

When you're constantly talking about the favor of God, bragging on His goodness, you will go places you couldn't go on your own. You will overcome obstacles that seem impossible. Maybe you've been single for a long time. You don't think you'll ever meet the right person. Start declaring, "The favor of God is bringing someone awesome into my life. Favor is making me attractive. Favor is putting me

> *When you're constantly talking about the favor of God, bragging on His goodness, you will go places you couldn't go on your own.*

at the right place at the right time." If you're struggling in your finances, instead of complaining, start declaring, "The favor of God is bringing increase and promotion. Favor is opening doors that I can't open. Favor is causing good breaks to come to me." Or the medical report doesn't look good. You could just pray about it, hope you get better, and that's good. But also start declaring, "The favor of God is bringing healing. The favor of God is causing me to recover. The favor of God is helping me to defy the odds. With long life, God will satisfy me."

Ever since I started ministering, I've said, "Father, thank You that Your favor causes me to stand out, that when people see me on television, they can't turn me off." Every week somebody tells me, "I was flipping through the channels. I don't like TV ministers. I never watch them, but, Joel, I turned you on, and I couldn't turn you off." I know that wasn't a coincidence. It wouldn't have happened if I had not declared favor.

Activate This Favor

The dreams that God has put in your heart, you need to speak favor over them. Those problems that look impossible, declare that the favor of God is turning them around. In the Scripture, Nehemiah had a dream to rebuild the walls around Jerusalem. They had been torn down, and the people living there were unprotected. This dream seemed impossible. Nehemiah was living a thousand miles from Jerusalem, working as a cupbearer to the king. He didn't have the influence, the connections, the resources, or the funding, but when God gives you a dream, He lines up everything you need. His favor will cause it to all come together. The question is, Are you going to activate this favor?

Nehemiah wasn't a cabinet member. He wasn't on the

king's executive staff. He was working in the kitchen, but he understood this principle: The favor on his life would help him accomplish dreams he couldn't accomplish on his own. He asked the king for permission to return to Jerusalem to work on the project. For some reason the king liked him. It didn't make sense to let him be gone that long, but the king said yes. Nehemiah said, "I'm going to need protection. Will you give me a letter addressed to all the leaders in the cities I'm traveling through, telling them who I am?" The king agreed. Nehemiah didn't stop there. He said, "One more thing, King. I don't have any supplies to rebuild the wall. I don't have any money. I need a letter from you that tells the people who own the lumber mills and the stone quarries to give me the materials I need." When you know you have favor, you'll have a boldness, a confidence to ask big, to expect advantages. Again the king said yes.

In Nehemiah 2, he said, "The king granted me these requests because the gracious hand of God was upon me." He was saying, "I know why all this happened. The favor of God is on my life." When you see God's favor, always take time to thank Him. Take a moment to say, "Lord, I recognize this was Your goodness. Thank You for favoring me. Thank You for making things happen that I couldn't make happen."

Nehemiah started on the wall, and he had all kinds of opposition, but every time the favor of God helped him to overcome. It should've taken him more than a year to

> *It's not going to take as long as you think to accomplish your dreams.*

rebuild it, but he did it in just fifty-two days. God's favor will accelerate things. It's not going to take as long as you think to accomplish your dreams, to recover from the illness, to pay off your house. The favor on your life is speeding things up. Nehemiah said, "I told all the people how the gracious hand of God was on my life." He was constantly bragging on God's goodness, constantly talking about His favor.

When you face situations that seem impossible, don't talk about how big the problem is. Do as Nehemiah did and start declaring, "The gracious hand of God is on my life." "Well, your child is off course." "Yes, but the favor of God is bringing him back." "You can't start your business. You don't have the connections." "Yes, but I have an advantage. The favor of God is bringing the right people to me." "Well, the medical report says you're done." "Yes, but I have another report. It says I will live and not die. Father, thank You that Your gracious hand is on me. Thank You that Your favor is doing what medicine cannot do." "Well, Joel, I tried this for two weeks, and nothing happened." No, this needs to be a way of life, where every day, whether it's sunny or rainy, whether you're on the mountaintop or in the valley, you get up in the morning and say, "I have the favor of God." That's not just to remind yourself, not just to show God that you're trusting Him, but you're showing the enemy who you belong to.

Crown Your Efforts with Success

The Scripture says, "If you will acknowledge God in all your ways, He will crown your efforts with success." One way to acknowledge God is, all through the day, under your breath, declare His favor. Before you make that presentation at work, say, "Father, thank You that I have favor with these people." Going to the mall, say, "Lord, thank You that Your favor will help me find what I need." The favor of God will help you get the best deals. Favor will put you at the right place at the right time. You pull into a crowded parking lot. Right when you drive in, a car backs out. You get that up-front spot. That wasn't a lucky break. That was the favor on your life.

Years ago I promised our daughter, Alexandra, that I would get her a cell phone. The next day she came running in and said, "Dad, can we go to the store?" I said yes. When Jonathan heard we were going, he wanted to come. I said, "That's great, Jonathan, because we'd love to have you, but you already have a cell phone." He said, "I know, Dad. I just want to look." Then when Victoria heard that we were all going, she decided to come along as well. It turned into a family affair. Driving to the store, under my breath, just out of habit, I said, "Lord, thank You for Your favor. Thank You that You'll help us find what we need." We walked into the store and a salesman came out to wait on us and showed us some phones. Alexandra found the one she wanted.

We were about to check out when Jonathan came over and said, "Dad, I really want the newer version of my phone." His phone was not even a year old, practically brand-new, and I really didn't want to do that. The salesman asked to see my phone, then he typed something into the computer and said, "You're due for an upgrade at no charge." I said, "Well, great. Give Jonathan the new phone, and I'll take his." His was like new to me. We were about to leave, but then the salesman said to Victoria, "What kind of phone do you have?" She showed him hers, and he said, "You need a new phone." He checked the computer, but she wasn't due for several years. I thanked him for checking and for all his help. As we were walking out, the store manager said, "Wait a minute. She's not leaving without a new phone." The salesman looked at the manager with an expression that said, "What do you mean? What do you want me to do?" He said, "Just give her a phone." The salesman's eyes got really big. He said, "You mean, like, give her, like, free, like, not charge her?" The manager said, "Yes, give her any phone she wants." We had gone in there to get one phone. We walked out with four, but we only paid for one. You may think that was good luck, but I know that's the favor of God.

Driving home, I reached my hand back to my children and said, "Come on, get some of this favor off me. I can't stand it all." When you not only recognize you have favor, but you declare favor, God will show out in your life. You will see things that you don't deserve. If you're in real estate, declare, "Father, thank You that Your favor is causing my properties to sell. Thank You that Your favor is bringing the right buyers." Before you take the exam at school, declare, "Father, thank You that Your favor is causing me to excel." Before you meet with those new clients, declare, "Lord, thank You that Your favor is making me attractive."

Ask for Rain

"Well, Joel, God's got bigger things to deal with than me getting a cell phone or finding a good parking spot." Can I tell you that you are God's biggest deal? You are the apple of His eye. He wants to show you His goodness. That's what favor is. The prophet Zechariah said, "Ask for rain in the time of rain." In the Scripture, rain represents favor. This seems odd. If it's raining, why do you need to ask for rain? God was saying, "Just because My favor is available, you're not going to experience it unless you call for it, unless you declare it." You may not be able to see it, but right now it's raining. It's raining healing, raining freedom, raining promotion, raining spouses, raining good breaks, raining abundance. God is showering His favor like never before. My challenge is, don't let it pass you by. Don't go around just hoping and believing. The way you get in the rain is by declaring favor: "Father, thank You that Your favor is opening doors

> *He wants to show you His goodness. That's what favor is.*

no man can shut. Thank You that Your favor is bringing good breaks, advantages, preferential treatment. Lord, thank You that Your favor is defeating enemies, turning negative situations around, breaking forces that are trying to stop me." Every time you declare favor, you're asking for the rain. That's what allows God to show out in your life.

I have friends whose son played on a minor league baseball team. His dream was to make it to the big leagues. He's extremely talented, led the division in hitting for several years, but it seemed as though every time he was about to get promoted to the big leagues, something would come up and he got passed over. His parents told me, again and again, how he was leading the league in home runs, how he was having a banner year, but for some reason he was overlooked. They could've been discouraged and thought it's not meant to be, but they did what I'm asking you to do. They kept declaring the favor of God: "Father, thank You that Your favor is on our son. Thank You that Your favor is putting him at the right place. Thank You that Your favor is causing him to stand out." The team he played for had a star player in the major leagues in his same position. It looked as if that player would be there for years, but one day, unexpectedly, the star player requested a trade and was sent to another team. This young man was suddenly promoted to the big leagues. He went on to live out his dream of playing Major League Baseball.

When you declare God's favor, He will move people out of the way to make room for you. Favor will promote you suddenly, unexpectedly, to things that you didn't see coming. You may not see how you can accomplish a dream or how you'll get well. It doesn't look as if it's ever going to change. I have good news. It's raining. If you'll do your part and keep declaring God's

> *Favor will promote you suddenly, unexpectedly, to things that you didn't see coming.*

favor, as with my friends' son, God is going to do something unusual, something that you weren't expecting, where suddenly you're promoted, suddenly you get well, or suddenly you meet the right person.

Don't Get Talked Out of Your Dreams

When we acquired the Compaq Center, we hired architects to draw plans to see what it would take to renovate it. We had to build our own power plant plus an additional five-story building. The cost came right at $100 million. We didn't have those kinds of funds, so we met with our bank to see what they would loan us. We had known these bankers for years, way back with my father. They knew the church's finances, how strong the ministry is, and the potential for growth. We met, and they were very nice, but they were as negative as can be. They told me all the reasons why it wasn't going to work out, how they could never take that kind of risk of loaning us that money, how every bank was going to say no, on and on. I left there so discouraged. I was young. I didn't know any better.

I've since learned that people don't have the final say. People don't control your destiny. People can't see the favor on your life. They don't know what God is about to do. Don't let them talk you out of your dreams. Don't let people convince you that you can't get well, you'll never afford a nice house, you'll never break the addiction. They're looking at the natural. We serve a supernatural God. One touch of His favor will catapult you ahead. They may be negative, discouraging, and condescending. Let it go in one ear and out the other. None of that can stop your purpose. The favor on your life will defy the odds. Favor will take you where you don't have the qualifications. On paper, it may not make sense. Don't worry. God knows what He's doing.

I woke up the next morning with a fire in my spirit. Something inside said, "Joel, God didn't bring you this far to leave you where you are. He didn't move the Rockets basketball out of that building, cause the mayor to be good to you, change a city council member's mind, and bring you through a lawsuit so you could get stuck where you are." I realized the favor of God had brought us that far, and the favor of God was going to keep us going. Instead of being discouraged, thinking, *Look how big these obstacles are*, my attitude was, *Look how big my God is. Father, thank You that Your favor is bringing the right people, people who will get behind the vision. Thank You that Your favor is making a way where I don't see a way.*

We decided to try another bank. We had never met these bankers, never had any contact with them, but when we walked in, it was a night-and-day difference. From the very beginning, they were for us. They had a letter on the table, offering us a loan three times the amount of what the other bank said we'd never get. They hadn't even seen our finances. They'd never looked at our books. When I saw they would loan us that much, I said, "How about loaning us the whole amount so we could do it all?" They said, "That won't be a problem. We'll make that happen."

God has these divine connections lined up for you, people who will be behind your vision, people who will be for you, not people you have to convince. You may not have seen them yet, but they are in your future. God has already ordained them to help you. The favor on your life is going to close the wrong doors and open the right doors. "Well, Joel, I've been declaring favor, but I don't see anything happening. It doesn't look like it's ever going to change." The apostle Peter says, "Hope to the end, for the divine favor that is coming." You may not have seen it yet, but favor is on the way. Healing is on the way. Promotion is on the way. The right people are on the way.

Mountains to Molehills

I met a man a few years ago who was so discouraged. He's in the graphic design industry. At one time his company had been very successful, but over the years, his business had gone down. He'd lost all his major clients. It looked as if bankruptcy was inevitable. He went on and on, telling me about the problem, going into great detail to explain all the setbacks he had suffered and how unfair it was. I finally had to interrupt him and say, "We've talked long enough about the problems. Let's start talking about the solution. Let's start talking about what God can do. Let's talk about the fact that favor is on the way." We prayed together. Then I said, "There's something you have to do. Every morning, you need to declare, 'I have the favor of God. Favor is bringing me new clients. Favor is turning my business around.' Then all through the day, under your breath, keep thanking God for that favor." I saw him several months later. He was like a new person, beaming with joy. He told how, at his lowest moment, when he thought he was done, a company that he had never worked for contacted him and asked him to make a presentation. They chose him over several major firms. He said, "With this one new client, I will have more income than from all my other clients combined." He was on pace to have a record year.

> *Every morning, you need to declare, "I have the favor of God."*

What you're facing may seem impossible. Don't talk about the problem. Talk about the solution. Talk about the fact that favor is on the way. "Yes, my finances may be low, but I know favor is coming." "These people at work aren't treating me right. I'm not going to live bitter. I know favor is on the way." "Well, my child is off course, but I know it's only temporary. The favor of God is turning it around."

This is what a man named Zerubbabel did in the Scripture. He was in charge of rebuilding the temple in Jerusalem. Everything came against him. City leaders hired attorneys to try to stop him; they wouldn't give him the permits. Other people were causing strife and trouble. It looked impossible. He could've been discouraged. But he heard the prophecy that the Lord gave to Zechariah about him, and based on that he said, "Who are you, O great mountain that stands before me? You shall become a mere molehill. I will finish the temple by shouting grace to it." He was saying, "I have this big mountain in front of me, but I'm not worried. I know it's about to become a molehill." How is this going to happen? What was his secret? By speaking grace to it. Another word for *grace* is *favor*. He was saying, "Yes, this obstacle is big, but I have the favor of God. Favor is making my crooked places straight. Favor is defeating my enemies. Favor is going to help me finish this project." He didn't talk *about* his mountain. He talked *to* his mountain.

When you face challenges, don't get discouraged. Speak favor over them. Look at your bank account and speak favor to it. "I will lend and not borrow. What I touch will prosper and succeed." Speak favor over your health. "This sickness is not the end. This pain is not permanent. The favor of God is bringing healing." Speak favor over the legal situation. "I will be victorious. The favor of God is keeping my enemies from defeating me." It's not enough to just pray about it. It's not enough to just believe. What's going to turn the mountain into a molehill is by speaking grace to it.

I want to make a declaration of favor over you. If you let this take root in your spirit, I believe chains that have held you back are going to be broken, and you're going to be released into a new level of your destiny. I declare that right now the favor of God is on your life in a new way. I declare favor over your family, favor over your marriage, favor over your finances. I declare favor at work, favor with your boss, favor with your colleagues, favor with your clients. I declare favor is opening new doors of opportunity, bringing promotion, increase, and abundance, causing the right people to be drawn to you. I declare favor over your health, strength, energy, wholeness. You are free from sickness, chronic pain, depression, and addictions. I speak favor over every force that's trying to stop you, and I declare that mountain is becoming a molehill. As with Nehemiah, God's favor is going to accelerate it. Things are going to happen sooner than you think. I declare the favor of God is going to catapult you to a new level. You're going to take new ground, set new standards, and reach the fullness of your destiny.

CHAPTER THREE

Favor Connections

When I was a teenager, I was pulled over by a police officer for driving too fast. When he read the name on my license, he asked if I was related to the pastor that he watched on television each week, and I told him that was my father. He returned my license, told me to slow down, and said I could go. I received favor because of who I was connected to. It wasn't anything I did. I just happened to be the son of a man who was favored, and because I was in relationship with him, his favor spilled over onto me.

The Scripture says, "Noah found favor with the Lord." When a great flood covered the earth, Noah's family was the only one saved. It never says his sons had favor or his daughters had favor, but because they were connected to Noah, their lives were spared. The principle is, when you're connected to people who are favored, people who are further along, people who are more successful, that favor is going to flow down to you. You'll see increase and promotion because of that association. There should be people you're in relationship with who inspire you, who challenge you, who make you strive to do better.

When you're connected to someone who's blessed, you honor them, you learn from them, you sow into them, and the more blessed they are, the more blessed you're going to be. Eventually, you're going to become like who you're connected to. The question is, Are you connected to anyone who has what you want, or are you connected to people who are negative, critical, can't get ahead, cause you to compromise, and drain your energy? It's fine to be a good influence. It's fine to encourage them. But if you're spending all your time with them, the problem is that you're going to become just like them. They're rubbing off on you.

You need to disconnect from people who are hindering your growth, limiting your potential, and causing you to compromise. Find some favor connections, people who are going places, people who are at a higher level, people who have what you're dreaming about. You need some eagles in your life. You cannot hang around with chickens and reach your destiny. You can't spend all your free time with crows, people who complain, or with turkeys, people who have accepted mediocrity. You need people who are soaring, people who are taking new ground, people who are out of debt, people who think bigger than you, people who are exposing you to levels that you've never seen.

Don't Have a Chicken Mentality

Several years ago I went to a meeting with a friend who runs television networks. They were negotiating a contract for programming. He said, "I want to offer $80 million." I almost fell out of my chair. I thought it was a big deal that we had spent $80,000 to buy a screen for the church. They talked about these huge numbers like I talked about buying a pair of tennis shoes. I didn't realize it, but God was expanding my vision. He was using that man to enlarge my thinking. After the meeting, I was about to tell him, "Wow! Those were some incredibly big numbers," but I felt something inside say, "Joel, zip it up."

When God puts you with a group of eagles, don't have a chicken mentality. Don't start talking about how you've never seen anything like that, how that could never happen for you. Let it take root inside. Breathe it in. Get used to it. That's where God is taking you. That's why He's exposing you to new levels—not to just impress you, not to just show you how the other half lives, but to get you prepared in your thinking. You have to make room for the new things God has in store. If you live with a limited vision, thinking, *It could never happen, it's too far out*, then you're right. It's not going to happen, because you'll never go where you can't accept it. But God gave you that favor connection to give you a glimpse into the next level, to show you where He's about to take you. Now do your part and get in agreement with God.

About five years after that meeting, we acquired the former Compaq Center, and when I found out it was going to cost about $120 million to purchase and renovate, I didn't fall apart. I wasn't intimidated. I thought, *God, You did it for my friend. You can do it for me.* But had I not connected with that man, had I only spent time with people at my level, I wouldn't be here. My mind wouldn't have been prepared. You need people who think bigger than you, who dream bigger, who believe bigger. If you're the smartest one in your group, your group is too small. God has already lined up these favor connections for you, people who are ordained to help you go further.

> *You need people who think bigger than you, who dream bigger, who believe bigger.*

Connect with Eagles

In the Scripture, Naomi and her daughter-in-law Ruth were both widows. They were living in Bethlehem, very poor. Ruth would go out into the harvest fields each morning and pick up leftover wheat. It looked as if this was their destiny, to just barely survive together. But Naomi saw a man named Boaz. He was the owner of all the fields, one of the wealthiest men in that area. She not only recognized the favor on his life, but she respected it. She told Ruth, "I want you to dress up, put on perfume, and go meet this man." She was saying, in effect, "Boaz has favor. We need to connect with him." Ruth not only met with Boaz, but they fell in love and eventually married, and because she connected with someone with favor, she had more favor than she ever imagined.

When you recognize the favor on a person's life, and you respect that favor by connecting with it, by honoring them and learning from them, that favor will come back to you. Naomi could have thought, *Oh, Boaz, he's wealthy, he's busy. He's not going to have anything to do with us.* She could've dismissed it and just stayed with the friends where she was comfortable. If she had, we wouldn't be talking about her today. She recognized Boaz was an eagle, and she was willing to get out of her comfort zone. No doubt, she had to break away from a few chickens, spend less time with a couple turkeys. She took these steps of faith and connected with an eagle. That's what opened new doors and took her and Ruth to a new level.

Are there favor connections God has put in your life that you're overlooking, people who have what you want, who are further along? Don't be intimidated by their success; be inspired. God put them there so you could connect. Their favor will flow down to you if you will honor and learn from them. Someone with more favor, more influence, and more vision, as with Boaz, can benefit you. You will see new doors open, influence in greater ways, promotion that you couldn't have reached on your own. It will come because of a favor connection.

What you sow into, you're going to reap. If you sow into worry connections, people who are always upset, anxious, and worried, you're going to reap worry. If you sow into compromise connections, people who are pulling you down, causing you to give in to temptation, you're going to reap compromise. If you

> *If you sow into these favor connections, into eagles, into people who are blessed, successful, and happy, that's what you'll reap.*

sow into gossip connections, critical connections, people who talk badly about the boss and complain about life, you're going to reap a negative, limited, discouraging life. But if you sow into these favor connections, into eagles, into people who are blessed, successful, and happy, that's what you'll reap. If you sow into people who have been where you want to go, who are out of debt, building orphanages, helping pay off other people's houses and expanding their businesses, you're going to reap favor, increase, and new levels.

We all have our friends. We have peers. Hopefully, we have people we're helping, people we're mentoring. That's important. But we should have a few of these favor connections, people who are far ahead of us. In the natural, it looks as though we could never get there. That connection is the seed God is going to use to take you where you've never dreamed.

Sow Honor, Respect, and Encouragement

A pastor friend of mine here in Houston had a church of several hundred people. He started it fifteen years ago, and they had been at that same number for years. It looked as though they had reached their limit and that's all they'd ever have. But he saw a pastor in California who had a large church, and he was so impressed by it that he flew out there just to attend a service. He sat in the auditorium, looked around, and breathed it all in. It was very inspiring. He had never seen anything that large. After the service, he was able to meet the pastor. He gave him a small donation that his church had taken up for their ministry. Then he started flying out to California every month just to attend a service and give a donation. He had plenty of pastor friends here in Houston. He had good members in his church and had a great family. But he understood that to reach a new level, you have to have some favor connections.

You need to be sowing time, energy, resources, and honor into people who have what you want. The anointing you respect is the anointing you will attract, and this pastor sowed into a vision much larger than his. He could have been jealous of the other pastor, intimidated, competitive. Instead, he celebrated what the minister was doing. He cheered him on. It wasn't long before his church started to grow. He went from 300 to 500, from 500 to 1,000, from 1,000 to several thousand. Now his church is larger than the church in California. He outgrew that man. I don't believe it would have happened if he had not sown into his ministry, and I don't mean just finances. He sowed honor, respect, and encouragement. He valued and esteemed what that man had built.

When we see people who are more successful, more talented, more blessed than us, it's easy to get jealous, try to compete, discredit them, talk about what they're doing wrong and how they're not talented. "They're just lucky." Here's a key: If you can't celebrate other people's success, you will never get to where they are. If you get jealous and try to outperform them, or if you're intimidated by them, you'll get stuck. It's a test. God brings these favor connections across our path. Are you secure enough in who you are to honor them, to respect them, to cheer them on, or will your pride keep you from connecting with their favor? The problem is, your destiny is tied to certain people. When you connect with the favor on their life, that's going to cause you to rise higher. But if we won't humble ourselves, if we think, *I'm as smart as them. I'm not going to celebrate them. They should be celebrating me*, that's going to limit our growth.

> *God brings these favor connections across our path.*

What you're connected to eventually is going to come back to you. Don't be small-minded, where you have to be the smartest one in your circle. If you're only sowing into your level, then your level is all that's going to come back. You need to sow into where you want to go. Swallow your pride and sow honor into that supervisor at work. Sow respect into that colleague who's really talented. They're not in your life by accident. God put them there as a favor connection. As you connect to them, new doors will open for you. New talents will come out, new levels. They are instrumental in you reaching the fullness of your destiny. But too often, when we see someone who's further along, someone who's more blessed, instead of being inspired, we get discouraged, thinking, *I could never get there.* God wouldn't have brought them across your path if He wasn't about to take you higher. The favor on their life is an indication of what God is about to do in yours.

Favor Will Flow Down on You

In the Scripture, when they poured oil on the head of Aaron, the high priest, it flowed down to the rest of his body. This is symbolic. Oil represents favor, and when you're connected to people with favor, the more blessed they are, the more blessed you'll be. That oil will flow down to you, and when we understand this, it's easy to celebrate those who are ahead. We know that because we're honoring them, sowing into them; as they rise higher, we're going to rise higher because we're connected. That favor is going to flow down to us, and as with that pastor, there will be times where you surpass who you're honoring. You overtake who you're celebrating.

When I first started ministering, I was very nervous and unsure of myself. I didn't have the training or the experience, but there were several very prominent ministers whom I knew from my growing up years. I listened to their messages over and over. I would send them notes telling them how much they had helped me, and how much I admired and respected them. One man in particular was a legend to me. He was so far ahead of me. I was amazed by what he had accomplished and how respected he was. I say this with humility, but now, nearly twenty years later, God has taken me further than him.

What am I saying? When you celebrate those who are ahead of you, when you show honor and respect, then some of the favor on them is going to come back to you. You'll look up and think, *How did I get here?* Part of it is the favor connection. You connected with someone who was where you wanted to go. That's why you don't have to compete with people. You don't have to try to outperform them. You're not in competition with anyone except yourself. Let where they are inspire you to be the best that you can be. As iron sharpens iron, they can sharpen you. They can make you better.

> *As iron sharpens iron, they can sharpen you. They can make you better.*

But when we start competing, before long we get jealous, find fault, and try to discredit others. Here's a key: Pulling somebody else down will never make you rise higher. Trying to make them look bad, spreading rumors, and magnifying their faults may feel good, but it's going to boomerang and come right back to us. If you sow disrespect, you'll reap disrespect. If you sow spreading rumors and stirring up trouble, that's what you'll reap. A much better approach is to celebrate those who are ahead. How do you know they're not a favor connection, somebody God brought into your life so you could rise higher? If you're jealous and competitive, you're letting what God meant for your good become something that's holding you back. Turn it around. Let's be people who celebrate success, who learn from those who are ahead, who honor people who are blessed with more influence.

Vertical Favor

In the Scripture, Elijah was a great prophet who did amazing miracles. One day he was walking by a field where he saw a young man named Elisha out plowing. He told Elisha to leave his team of oxen and come with him. But Elisha came from a well-to-do family. I'm sure he had goals and dreams. Elijah wanted him to become his assistant, which basically meant to take care of him, bring him food, set up his tent, and feed his animals. Elisha could've thought, *No, thanks. I'll stay here at my own place.* He could've been too proud, but he recognized the favor on Elijah's life. He respected his anointing. He wasn't jealous. He didn't get bitter when Elijah offered him what seemed to be a low-level position.

For years Elisha served Elijah with honor, watching after him and making sure he was comfortable. When you sow into someone with great favor, you're going to reap some of that favor. When you honor someone who has more influence, some of that influence is going to come back to you. I'm sure Elisha's friends came around and said, "Elisha, what are you still doing here, serving this old man? You have your own dreams. Why don't you start your own ministry? He's holding you back." He could've let them talk him out of his position, to convince him that he was wasting his time, but he just kept on sowing, honoring, and respecting the favor connection.

Eventually, when Elijah was taken to heaven in a whirlwind, Elisha received a double portion of Elijah's anointing. He didn't just get the favor on Elijah's life; he got twice the favor. Remember that with some of these favor connections that you're sowing into, giving to, serving and honoring, your time is coming. As with Elisha, you're not just going to go to the level where they are. You're going to go further and have double the influence, double the favor, double the resources.

This is why the enemy works overtime to try to get us jealous of one another, competing and trying to pull one another down. He wants us to get stuck where we are. It's very freeing when you can celebrate those who are ahead, knowing that the seeds you sow into them—the honor, the respect, the resources—are going to come back to you. But if you're only sowing into horizontal relationships, into people who are at your level, then you're going to see horizontal favor. When you're secure enough in who you are to sow into vertical relationships, into people who are ahead of you, you're going to reap some of this vertical favor.

> *When you're secure enough in who you are to sow into vertical relationships, into people who are ahead of you, you're going to reap some of this vertical favor.*

Recognize Your Favor Connections

Many pastors sow into our ministry. They faithfully support and attend our events. They tell me again and again how, when they connected with us, their church started growing in new ways. One man told me that his church has gone from 200 people to over 6,000 people. He said, "Joel, I can pinpoint the exact time it started. It was when we connected with you at your Night of Hope in our city."

I'm not bragging. This is a spiritual principle. God has people in your life who are favor connections. You could be one relationship away from a new level. Look around, find the people whom God is blessing, and connect with them. Don't be intimidated or jealous. If you honor, respect, and sow into them, that favor will come back to you.

I know a man who had a dream of being in the hospitality business. He wanted to own hotels. When he was eighteen, he met an older gentleman who owned one of the largest hotel chains in the world. He convinced that man to give him a job working as a bellman at one of his hotels. Every time this young man saw the owner, he went overboard to take care of him, opening the door and carrying his briefcase, constantly sowing, honoring, and respecting. The owner loved this young man and kept promoting him. In his early thirties, he left to start his own business. There was a piece of very expensive real estate that overlooked the ocean on which this owner was planning to build a big hotel.

This young man came to the owner and asked if he could buy that property from him. This was the prime location where they were planning on this big project. It had taken them over ten years to acquire it. The owner said, "I never dreamed I would do this, but you have been so good to me that I want you to be successful. I'm going to sell you this property." That young man built a beautiful resort that is incredibly successful. Today he has hotels all over the world. It all started when he recognized a favor connection.

> *There are people God has put in your life, not to compete with but to connect with.*

There are people God has put in your life, not to compete with but to connect with. They will be instrumental in you rising higher, and this is not about playing up to people, trying to win them over. It's about recognizing and respecting the favor that God's placed on people.

Your Boat Is Going to Be Full

In Luke 5, Jesus borrowed Peter's boat so He could teach a large crowd of people who were gathered on the shore. When He finished, He told Peter to launch out into the deep and he would catch a great haul of fish. Peter had fished all night and caught nothing, but he went back out to try it again. He caught so many fish that his nets began to break and, it says, "Peter shouted for help, and his partners came." Soon both boats were so loaded with fish that they were concerned the boats might sink. Peter was blessed because he obeyed. He had favor. But notice, the favor didn't stop with him. He caught so many fish that his partners, those who were connected with him, received the overflow. When you connect with someone who's blessed, someone who's favored, as they increase, you'll increase. Peter's partners hadn't done anything to deserve the fish. Peter was the one who lent Jesus the boat. God could have just sent enough fish to fill Peter's boat and made sure Peter was paid back, but God blessed Peter on purpose in such a way that there would be overflow so all in partnership, all those connected, would see increase and favor as well.

Who you're connected to is extremely important. There are blessings that belong to you that are attached to the people God has placed in your life, and if you're not seeing any fish, you need to evaluate who you're connected to. You may need to disconnect from relationships that aren't producing any increase and connect with people who are blessed, people who are seeing favor. Peter's boat was not only full of fish, but his partner's boat was full of fish.

You're going to become like whoever you're connected to. Are you connected to anyone who has what you want, people who are more blessed, people who are more successful? Look around and find the favor connections in your life. Don't be intimidated because they're further along. Don't be jealous because they have more. Celebrate them, honor them, and sow into them. If you do this, I believe and declare, because you're connected to favor, as with Peter's friends, your boat is going to be full. You're going to see increase, promotion, and new levels. It's headed your way!

CHAPTER FOUR

Distinctive Favor

The favor God puts on your life causes you to be different. It's a favor that makes a distinction between you and those who don't honor God. The Scripture speaks of how you've been called out, set apart. Some older translations say you are "a peculiar people." I think a better phrase is "a different people." You're not ordinary; you're not like everyone else. You've been marked with a distinction. Numbers 6 says that God's face will shine down on you and cause you to stand out.

This distinctive favor causes you to prosper when others are struggling. You recover from a difficulty when others get stuck. You have protection when others face calamity. There's a marked difference. You have an advantage. You're not doing life by yourself, just on your own strength, your talent, your connections. There is a force breathing behind you, guiding you, protecting you, favoring you. The Most High God has set you apart. He could have chosen anyone, but He handpicked you, called you out, and said, "That's one of Mine." Right now, His face is shining down on you. Don't go through life thinking that you're average, that you can never accomplish your dreams. Put your shoulders back. Hold your head high. You're a part of the called-out group.

God has set you up for a distinctively favored life. That means He's set you up for blessings you didn't work for, for promotion you didn't deserve. The Scripture says, "For houses you didn't build, for vineyards you didn't plant." It's not because of who you are; it's because of Whose you are. You've been marked with favor. When you realize this, you'll pray bold prayers. You'll dream big dreams. You'll expect things to happen for you that may not happen for others. When others are afraid and upset and worried, you'll be at peace, knowing that you've been set apart, that there's a hedge around you that the enemy cannot cross, that you have distinctive favor.

> *It's not because of who you are; it's because of Whose you are.*

A Hedge of Protection

When the Israelites were in slavery, God told Moses to go and tell Pharaoh to let His people go. But Pharaoh wouldn't listen. He kept refusing. God sent plague after plague on Pharaoh and his people. Their water supply was turned to blood. Millions of flies made their lives miserable, and swarms of locusts ate their crops and destroyed their land. What's interesting is that the Israelites, some two million people, lived right next door, but these plagues never affected them. At one point, there were hordes of frogs. Everywhere Pharaoh's people looked there were frogs—in their homes, in their food, in their beds. They were so frustrated. On the Israeli side there were no frogs. Life went on as usual. But Pharaoh still wouldn't change his mind.

When God was about to send swarms of flies into the Egyptian houses, He said to Pharaoh, "I will deal differently with the land where My people live. No swarms of flies will be there. I will make a distinction between you and My people." Millions and millions of flies came into Pharaoh's palace and all the houses of the Egyptians. The flies were so dense the people couldn't see, couldn't eat, couldn't sleep. Their land was ruined by flies. But right next door, the Israelites had no flies. I can hear the Israelites saying to their neighbors, "I'll let you borrow my fly swatter. We don't need it over here." It didn't make sense in the natural. This was the hand of God putting a distinction on His people.

God has put that same distinction on you. When He breathed life into you, He marked you for favor, marked you for blessing, marked you to stand out. What will defeat others won't be able to defeat you. This is why you don't

> *What will defeat others won't be able to defeat you.*

have to live worried—worried about your safety, worried about your future, worried about your children—even though there are so many negative things in the world, so much crime and violence. It may be happening all around you, but you have an advantage. God has put a distinction on you. The psalmist said, "A thousand may fall at my side, ten thousand at my right hand, but it will not come near me." God has placed a hedge of protection around you and your family. For the enemy to get to you, he has to ask God for permission.

I'm not saying negative things will never happen. That's not reality. I'm saying you are protected by the One who controls it all. If God allows it to happen, He's promised that He will turn it somehow and use it for your good.

Marked for Distinction

Pharaoh still wouldn't let the Israelites go after the plague of flies. Then Moses told him, "There's about to be a plague on all your livestock, your horses, camels, goats, and sheep." But once again, the Scripture says God put a distinction on the livestock of the Israelites so that not one of the Israelites' animals would die. Notice a distinction is even on your property—your house, your car, your belongings. The next day, just as God had said, all their oppressors' livestock died, but not one animal belonging to the Israelites.

I'm sure some of Pharaoh's people thought, *That's it. I'm going to the Israeli side. These frogs, flies, and locusts are making my life miserable.* They moved over to the Israelites' land, set up temporary homes...but everywhere they went, the plagues followed them. It wasn't where the Israelites were that kept them from the plagues. It was what was on them—the distinction, the favor, the blessing that comes from being a child of the Most High God.

You and I have that same blessing. We may have things around us that could harm us, keep us from our dreams, bring us down. Stay in faith. There is a distinction on your life, on your property, on your children, on your career, and on your health that is put there by the Creator of the universe.

When I was growing up, a friend of ours was a successful businessman who owned hundreds of acres of orange groves. One winter day, it was predicted that there was going to be a hard freeze, which was unusual in that part of the country. It almost never froze there. He knew the freeze would destroy all his crops and cost him thousands of dollars. In the natural, there was nothing he could do. That's what all the circumstances said. But he understood this principle that God had put a distinction on his property, that God had a hedge around his business. Instead of being defeated, thinking, *Oh, great! Bad luck this year*, he went out and walked all around his orange groves, thanking God that his trees would live, thanking Him that they wouldn't freeze and that he would have a harvest that year. When the other farmers who lived around him heard what he did, that he prayed for his trees, they thought he was so strange, so far out. They made fun and ridiculed him.

The next day the big freeze came in and lasted a little over twenty-four hours. The other farmers were very discouraged, trying to figure out how they were going to make a living, not having a harvest that year. But a couple weeks later, there was the most unusual sight. Our friend's property, hundreds and hundreds of acres, had the most beautiful, healthy orange trees. The trees on the properties next to his, on all four sides, were totally dead. It was as though somebody had put a blanket over our friend's property. The other farmers were so amazed that instead of making fun of him, they asked him, "Next time will you pray for our crops as well?"

I know some people will think, *Joel, that's just a lucky break. That's just the way the clouds must have formed that day, just the way the winds must have blown.* No, that was the hand of God putting a distinction on his property. That was God's face shining down on him. God has put this same distinction on you. Don't talk yourself out of it. "Well, business is slow. A couple of my coworkers got laid off. I don't see how I can get out of debt." Your job is not your source. God is your source. The economy doesn't determine whether or not you're blessed; God does. He has already marked you for favor. He's already put this distinction on your life. Dare to pray bold prayers. Believe for unusual favor. Take the limits off God. You've been set apart.

A Supply Line That Never Runs Dry

A lady told me how she was having her best year in her career. She works in a sales position, and her whole industry in general was down. They were going through a transition. Her coworkers were struggling, and her competitors were way down. But she said, "It seems as though every time I turn around, a new account is finding me." She told how on three or four occasions she was at the right place at the right time. Unexpectedly, business dropped into her lap. She made the statement, "Joel, I'm supposed to go out and find new customers, but it's as if new customers are always finding me." Psalm 37 says, "Even in famine, the righteous will have more than enough." Even in a downtime, because she's the righteous, because she has this distinction, she's seeing increase and favor.

Here's the key: As long as you stay close to God, as long as you keep Him first place, you are connected to a supply line that will never run dry. Even in a slow economy, God will cause clients to find you. Even when the medical report says no way, you are connected to a supply line filled with health, wholeness, and restoration. When you don't see how you can accomplish your dreams, don't get discouraged. You have a supply line connected with good breaks, the right people, ideas, and creativity.

I have friends who live in another state, and they were trying to sell their home, but the housing market in their area was very depressed. A large company nearby had gone out of business, and that's where many of their neighbors worked. Now there was a surplus of homes on the market. On their street alone, there were twelve houses for sale.

The average time for a house to sell back then was a year and a half. Their Realtor had already told them, "Don't be in a hurry. This is going to be a long, drawn-out process, and the value could go down and down." In the natural, it didn't look good. But instead of expecting the worst, thinking their house would never sell, this young couple was bold enough to believe that God had put a distinction on their property like He did for the Israelites. Every morning they said, "Father, thank You that You're causing our house to stand out. Thank You that people are being drawn to it." Six weeks after they put the house on the market, they received a contract and sold it. At the closing, they were talking to the new owners, who said they had looked at many different properties, even houses that were a better value and in a better location. But they said, "When we came to your house, there was just something different about it. We felt a peace. We knew it was supposed to be ours."

What is that? Distinctive favor, where God causes it to stand out. I wonder what would happen if you would get up every morning and say, "Father, thank You that Your face is shining down on me. Thank You that You put a distinction on my life." All the circumstances may say otherwise. "You'll never get well. You'll never meet the right person. Your house is never going to sell." Don't believe those lies. You have to have a boldness like this young couple to believe that there's something different about you, that you have a right to be blessed, you have a right to see favor. I don't mean arrogantly, but in humility, knowing that because of who you are, a child of the Most High, He has set you apart, He's put favor on you that causes you to stand out. Like the Israelites, God has put a distinction on your life, on your property, on your career. You have an advantage. If you get this down in your spirit, you'll start praying these bold prayers and believing for things that seem impossible.

> *Like the Israelites, God has put a distinction on your life.*

Keep Rising to the Top

This is what my father did. He tried for many years to build a new church sanctuary, but every time he tried to move forward, he felt an unrest, knowing it wasn't the right time. In 1986, Houston was in one of the deepest recessions our city had ever seen. Businesses were going bankrupt. People were struggling. My father had just been released from the hospital after having open-heart surgery. It was a few weeks before Christmas. It seemed like the worst time to start any project, especially the worst time to try to raise funds. Deep down he could hear God telling him to do it right then. But he thought, *God, that doesn't make sense. This is a downtime. People aren't going to have extra income. How can we possibly raise these funds?* He heard God whisper, "Son, I want you to do it now so people will know it's Me and not anybody else."

God likes to do unusual things in your life so others

will be drawn to Him. A year and a half later, they dedicated a new six-million-dollar auditorium totally debt free. Even in a down economy, even when critics said no way and circumstances said it's not going to happen, God said, "Don't worry. It may be that way in the natural, but I'm a supernatural God. I put a distinction on you that will cause you to defy the odds, to have more than enough even in famine."

In the Scripture, Joseph went through a lot of bad breaks. He was betrayed by his brothers, sold into slavery, put in prison for something he didn't do. For thirteen years, you could say, he was in a famine. He could have been bitter and negative. "God, why did You let this happen to me?" But Joseph understood this principle. Despite the opposition, he kept being his best. No matter how much people tried to push him down, he kept rising to the top. He worked for a man by the name of Potiphar. Joseph was so excellent in what he did, he had such a good attitude, that Potiphar put him in charge of his household. The Scripture says that Potiphar noticed the Lord was with Joseph, giving him success in everything he did. Potiphar saw the distinction.

God wants to bless you in such a way that people notice. He wants to show out in your life to where people say, "You mean you sold your house in six weeks when it should have taken a year and a half? You mean all the orange groves froze, but yours didn't? You mean you built the sanctuary in the middle of a recession? Joel, you mean your mother had terminal cancer in 1981, but she's still alive today? You mean you're having church in the former Compaq Center?"

That's what distinctive favor does. It causes you to stand out. You may have seen some of this in the past, but you need to get ready. You haven't seen anything yet. God is about to do some things in your life that are going to get you noticed. People are going to see it wasn't just your talent, your ability, your connections. It was the hand of God opening doors that no man can open, taking you where you could not go on your own.

The Scripture says God began to bless Potiphar for Joseph's sake. Because of the distinction on Joseph's life, people around him began to get blessed. Your company should be glad to have you at work. When you get there, the blessing gets there. When you show up, favor shows up. Some of your friends, relatives, and coworkers don't even know they're being blessed because of you.

> *Because of the distinction on Joseph's life, people around him began to get blessed.*

What's interesting is that Joseph was a slave. He didn't have a prestigious position. He was taking care of the household, doing repairs, mowing, cleaning. On the other hand, Potiphar was one of the highest-ranking military officials of that day. People looked up to him, saluted him, and did whatever he commanded. You would think that Joseph would be blessed for Potiphar's sake. It was just the opposite.

What am I saying? The distinction God put on you is more powerful than positions, than titles, than education. When God's face is shining down on you, you'll not only rise higher, but it's so powerful that even the people around you will begin to get blessed.

I know a man who used to do some consulting work with us years ago. We were a small client compared to most of his clients. He consulted for the big Fortune 500 companies and had a really impressive résumé. We got to know each other and went out to lunch a couple times. After about a year, he said, "Joel, ever since I started working for your ministry, my business has gone to a new level." He named client after client that he had picked up—big, impressive names. He turned to the associate standing next to us and said, "I like working for Joel. He brings me good luck." He called it "luck," but I know it's the distinction God puts on our life. It's the favor He's placed on you and me.

Your Location Doesn't Determine the Blessing

In the Scripture, when Abraham moved to a new country with his family, his nephew Lot, and all his flocks and herds, he found a beautiful piece of land, with luscious green pastures and peaceful ponds. It looked like a postcard. But after a few months, he realized the land couldn't sustain all the flocks and herds. He told Lot to choose where he wanted to live with his flocks and herds, and Abraham would take his and go elsewhere. Lot said he wanted to stay right there, in the best part of the land. Instead of arguing, Abraham took the high road and moved to a different part of the country. But this time, all he could find was land that was dry and barren. Instead of lush, beautiful green pastures, it was more like the desert, with rocks and sand and very little water.

In the natural, Abraham should have struggled. He should have seen his crops dry up and his business go down to nothing. But it was just the opposite. Hardly any time passed before his flocks and herds multiplied so much and that dry barren land had turned into a beautiful oasis. In fact, the Scripture speaks of how he had so much that he became one of the wealthiest men of that time.

As with Abraham, even if you're in the desert, because of the distinction God put on you, you're still going to flourish. Your location doesn't determine the blessing. What God put on you determines the blessing. When He called you out, He marked you for favor. Wherever you go, the blessing goes. You might not have the perfect job, people might not be treating you right, and you might not be getting the credit you deserve. That's okay, because you're not working unto people, you're working unto God. People don't determine your destiny; God does. Keep being your best, honoring God, and as with Joseph, God will cause you to be noticed. He'll cause you to stand out.

> *Wherever you go, the blessing goes.*

Potiphar will come looking for you. At the right time, God will either turn that around by promoting you, or He'll move you somewhere else.

But the key is to not think that you can wait until you're out of the desert and then you're going to have a good attitude, then you're going to start being your best. There's something on you right now that will cause you to prosper in the middle of the desert. Lot wasn't making good decisions. He wasn't honoring God. He was blessed as long as Abraham was there, but when Abraham left, the blessing left. Lot's fields dried up. His flocks went down to nothing. He ended up leaving that place. Eventually, Abraham had to go and rescue him and his family.

As with Lot, there are people whom God put into your life right now who are being blessed because of you. They may never realize it. They may never tell you thank you. Don't worry, because God is keeping the records. Those are seeds that you're sowing. He'll make sure you are blessed in a greater way. Back then, they would even pray to the God of Abraham. When they saw how blessed Abraham was, how he flourished even in the desert, they thought, *If we can get to his God, maybe we'll be blessed.* God wants to put such a distinction on you. He wants you to stand out in such a way that people want what you have. They'll say, "I'm going to pray to the God of those people at Lakewood. I'm going to pray to the God of Robert, to the God of Susan, to the God of Maria. Look at how blessed she is, so faithful, so generous, so talented. If I can get to her God, I believe I can be blessed."

This Favor Accelerates Your Dreams

I received an email from a lady named Ruby. One night after dinner, she and her husband, George, took the leftovers out of their refrigerator and were playing with different recipes to make gumbo. They were trying different combinations, different spices, just having fun, seeing what they could create. They came up with a recipe they liked so much that they started selling it door to door. It was a big hit. Everyone loved their gumbo. One night they saw a television commercial about a large grocery store chain that was looking for contestants for a cooking competition. Whoever won would get to put their product on these stores' shelves. They sent their gumbo in, and out of six hundred submissions, they were notified that they made it into the top twenty-five. They were so excited. They kept praying and believing.

A few months later the grand prize winner was announced, but unfortunately it wasn't them. It was as if the wind had been taken out of their sails. They attend Lakewood, and I'd just spoken about how God strategically orchestrates our steps, how He doesn't always take us in sequence from A to B to C. Sometimes He'll take you two steps ahead, one step back, and then five steps forward. The key is to trust

Him in those times when it feels like you're going in the wrong direction.

Several months later, Ruby was in our Wednesday night service when she received a phone call from her contact at that grocery store chain. She went out into the lobby and answered it. They said, "Even though you didn't win, we like your gumbo so much that we still want to put it on our shelves." She and George were thrilled. They couldn't believe it.

But part of this distinction is that God wants to accelerate your dreams coming to pass. He's going to speed things up, make it happen faster than you thought. After the store chain had carried the gumbo for a short time, they called again and said, "Your gumbo is so great that we want you to create a whole food line for us, and we'll help you get it started." In less than a year, this couple went from one night of playing in their kitchen with leftovers to having the availability to create a food line in one of the largest grocery store chains around.

God knows how to get you noticed. His face is shining down on you right now. He's put a distinction on your life, your property, your career, your children. It's going to cause you to stand out. It's going to open doors that you could never open. It's going to bring opportunity, the right people, and good breaks. You're not doing life alone. You have the most powerful force in the universe breathing in your direction right now. You've been called out, set apart, chosen to live a distinctively favored life. Now do your part. Pray bold prayers. Take the limits off God. Believe for your dreams. If you do this, I believe and declare that God is going to show out in your life in amazing ways. As with Abraham, you will prosper in a desert. As with Joseph, He's going to cause you to be noticed. And as with this last couple, it's going to happen faster than you think.

CHAPTER FIVE

God Is Your Source

It's easy to look to people as our source or to look to our job as our source. Yes, God uses people, He uses jobs, and He uses contracts, but they are not the Source. They are simply a resource that the Source uses. If you're seeing things other than God as your source, the problem is that if something happens to them, you'll think, *What am I going to do? The source has been cut off.* No, the Source is just fine. God is still on the throne. The Scripture says, "Every good gift comes from our Father in heaven above." That good gift may come through people, but it came from God. Your salary may come through your company, but it came from your heavenly Father. He's the One who caused that company to hire you. He's using them as a resource. That contract may have come through a friend or through another connection, but it came from God.

That's why you don't have to play up to people at work or compromise to get a good break. People are not your provider; God is your provider. That job is simply the resource through which God chose to bless you. If you don't understand this, you can make people your God. "If my supervisor doesn't like me, if this contract doesn't last, if this client is not good to me, how will I make it?" Take people off the throne. People are not your source; God is your source. It's nice when they're good to you, it's nice when they recognize your value, but don't become so dependent on them that you start seeing them as your provider. Recognize that behind the resource is the Source. Behind the income and behind the opportunity is the Most High God causing people to be good to you, causing that door to open, causing that client to seek you out. Be grateful for the resource, but keep your eyes on the Source.

When Peter didn't have money to pay his taxes, Jesus told him to go to the lake and catch a fish. The first fish he caught had a gold coin in it, enough to pay his taxes. God was showing us how He can use different resources. If a contract runs out at work and it looks as though you're going to be set back, don't be discouraged. God has another fish. He has things you've never thought of. When you keep God first place, you're connected to a supply line that will never run dry. You're not at the mercy of the economy, or who likes you, or what your boss does. God has all kinds of resources He can use.

Are You Recognizing the Source?

I talked to a man who had worked thirty-two years for the same company when it was suddenly sold and he was out of a job. He was so discouraged. He never dreamed that at his age he would have to start over. I told him what I'm telling you: That job was simply the resource God was using to bless you. It's not the Source. The Source is still fine, and He already has another resource lined up. About six months later this man came back so happy. He said, "I didn't just get another job, but I got a position that I've always dreamed of." Now his income was almost double. The benefits were better, and his workplace was closer to his home.

When a door closes, when you have a setback, you have to remind yourself that the resource is not what's blessing you; it's the Source. The Scripture says that even in the desert you will prosper, your leaf will not wither; even in a famine you will have more than enough. It's showing us that even though circumstances may change, the Source never changes. Because you're connected to the Source, God, you will be blessed in the famine, you'll increase when others are decreasing. All through the day you should say, "Lord, I recognize You're the Source of my life. Yes, this job gives me a paycheck, but You're the Source of the income. This company gave me a job, but You're the Source of this favor."

> *Even though circumstances may change, the Source never changes.*

In Chapter Three, I stated that Ruth and her mother-in-law, Naomi, came to recognize that Boaz was their favor connection. When Ruth found out that Boaz had told his workers to leave handfuls of grain on purpose for her, I can hear her telling Naomi, "The man Boaz, who is the owner, is being so good to me. He's leaving me so much wheat." She thought it was Boaz who was showing her favor; the truth is, it was God being good to her. Boaz was the resource, but God was the Source. God spoke to Boaz and caused him to want to be good to her. How many times has God spoken to people to be good to us and we didn't know it? For no apparent reason they decided to help us. They opened a door, gave us a position, or introduced us to a friend. They were a resource that the Source was using.

The longer I live the more I recognize the goodness of God in my life. I realize how things I thought were a coincidence, such as people just deciding to be good to me, were actually from the Source. When doors opened that you couldn't open, when somebody decided to give you a good break, when you were at the right place at the right time, when you met that person and fell in love, that wasn't a coincidence; that was the Source. You weren't being lucky when that person put in a good word for you and you got that promotion. God spoke to that person as He did to Boaz, telling them to be good to you. Every good thing comes from your Father. They may not have even known it was God, thinking they just suddenly had the desire to help you—to stay late and introduce you to that friend, or to wave the policy and put the loan through. Are you recognizing the Source? Are you thanking God for every good thing?

Do you realize that you wouldn't have awakened this morning without the Source, you wouldn't have air to breathe without the Source, your eyes couldn't see without the Source, you wouldn't have money for gas in your car without the Source, you wouldn't have the strength to read this book without the Source, you wouldn't have that person to love without the Source? Don't get so caught up in the resources that you forget it was God breathing on your life, it was God protecting you on the freeway from that accident, it was God healing you from that cancer and not just the medicine—it was the Source. It was God causing you to conceive those children whom you adore. When you look back over your life, there were no lucky breaks, there were no coincidences. What you thought was Boaz just being good to you, just leaving handfuls of grain on purpose—that was the hand of God. That was the Source at work behind the scenes, telling them to be good to you.

A Resource the Source Uses

When we were trying to acquire the Compaq Center, the building was owned by the city. So we had to get the city council members to vote to approve it. I had never been involved in any kind of politics, or in the need for convincing council members. I thought that was way out of my area of expertise. I had no experience in it. Someone randomly introduced us to a man who had been in city politics for most of his life and had worked for different mayors for many years. He wasn't the typical white-collar professional

you might envision. He was a bit on the rough side, liked
to party, liked to drink, didn't always use good language.
But for some reason he really liked us and wanted us to
get the building.

This man went overboard to make things happen. He
used his favor, all of his influence, to sway people. When
one council member was against us, he said, "Don't worry.
He owes me. He'll vote for you." I didn't ask for any of
the details. I just said, "Thank You, Jesus." This man had
never been in church his whole life, but he was doing all
he could to help Lakewood get the building. I look back
now and realize that wasn't just him deciding to help us,
that wasn't just him deciding to do a good deed. He was a
resource whom the Source was using. That was God working
behind the scenes. God was talking to him and he didn't
even know it, putting in him that desire to help us.

After we got the building, he came to one of our services.
When he was being interviewed years later about the building and why he helped us, he said, "I don't go to church.
I went to Lakewood one time, and I don't like the circus."
(Yes, our services are kind of loud and fun, but we've never
brought elephants in, Victoria's never walked the high wire,
and my brother, Paul, has never been shot out of a cannon.)
He went on to say—and I'm not telling you this to brag
on me but to make a point—"I helped them because I've
never met anyone like Joel. I would walk through a fire for
that man." I'd like to think I'm that charming and that
dynamic, but can I tell you I'm not? I didn't even really

know him. That's the Source; that's God putting the right people in our path, that's God causing someone to go out of their way to be good to us.

Gather as Many Containers as You Can

In 2 Kings 4, there's the story of a woman and her husband who were friends with the prophet Elisha, but the husband died. Years passed, and eventually she didn't have any money to pay her bills. Things had gotten so bad that the creditors were coming to take her two sons as payment. You can imagine how distraught she was. Elisha came by and she told him what was happening. He asked her what she had in her house. Her first answer was, "Nothing at all." She was saying, "Elisha, I'm done. It's too late. All the odds are against me." Sometimes we look at what we have compared to what we need and we think as she did: *I'll never accomplish my dreams. I don't have what I need. I'll never get out of debt, never get well, never meet the right person.* We're looking only at the resources, the circumstances, the bank account, the medical report. The resources may have dried up, but the Source is still alive and well.

The woman finally said, "Elisha, I do have one thing in my house, but really it's nothing, just a small jar of olive oil." She thought, *Why should I even mention that? I have a huge debt, and all I have is something that's worth a few dollars.* Don't discount the small thing that you have—the small opportunities, the small income, the small gifts. It may seem too small, but God knows how to multiply. The Scripture says, "When you have faith the size of a mustard seed, which is one of the smallest seeds, you can say to this mountain 'move,' and it will move." God doesn't expect us to have great faith all the time. It's nice when we do, but God is so merciful. He knows there will be times like this when we think it's impossible. If you just say, "God, all I have is this little bit

> *If you just say, "God, all I have is this little bit of oil, all I have is mustard seed faith," then watch what God will do.*

of oil, all I have is mustard seed faith," then watch what God will do.

Elisha told her to go borrow as many large containers as she could find. I can see her knocking on one neighbor's door after another, carrying those containers back home. Don't you know that God saw her faith? God saw her being obedient, doing what she could. When you're in difficult times, don't sit around in self-pity. Do something where God can see your faith. Make plans to get well, make plans to come out of that trouble, make plans for God to show out in your life. Have you gathered any containers? Have you taken any steps to show God that you're ready to see His favor? Have you done what He's asking you to do? I can hear her neighbors asking her, "Why do you need all these containers when you don't have anything to put in them? All you have is that little bit of olive oil." She answered, "I don't have it yet, but I know it's on the way. I know the prophet wouldn't have told me to do it if God wasn't up to something."

Faith started to rise in her heart. All the circumstances were against her; friends were trying to talk her out of what she was doing, and her own thoughts were telling her that she was wasting her time and it was never going to work out. Her attitude was, *I'm connected to a supply line that will never run dry. God is my source. He's my provider.*

Elisha told her to pour the little bit of oil into the first container. That didn't make sense. What good was it going to do to just transfer the oil from one container to another? What God asks us to do, many times, is more about the obedience than the actual thing we're doing. It's a test. If you obey, you'll see God's favor.

In another story that involved Elisha, a man named Naaman was a captain in the enemy's army but he had leprosy. When he came to Elisha for help, Elisha told him to wash in the Jordan River seven times and he would be healed. Naaman was offended and came up with all these excuses about why he didn't want to do it: "The water is dirty. We have better rivers back home." He almost talked himself out of it, but finally he did as Elisha had instructed. When he came up out of the water the seventh time, his skin was perfectly normal. The healing wasn't in the water, it was in the obedience. Are you doing what God is asking you to do? Are you gathering the containers, are you pouring the oil?

This woman could have talked herself out of it, thinking,

I'm not going to waste my time pouring this oil. She would have missed the miracle. When she poured the oil into the first container, the oil never stopped flowing. She filled up the first one, then the second, then the third. That didn't make sense. Where was the oil coming from? The Source. When you do what God asks you to do even when it doesn't make sense, God will do things for you that don't make sense. He'll show out in your life. This lady kept pouring until all the containers were full of oil. Then she went and sold the oil and had enough money to pay her bills with plenty left over to live on. That little bottle should have run out, but God has supernatural provision. He knows how to not only sustain you but increase you, to where you defy the odds.

Supernatural Flow

You may have areas in your life that are dry, where you haven't seen any good breaks, any increase, any favor. It seems like it's permanent. Get ready. Things are about to flow again. God is about to do something unusual, something out of the ordinary. You can't make it happen, the odds are against you, but the Source is going to send a supernatural flow. It may look as though that dream has dried up, but favor is about to flow, finances are about to flow, good breaks are about to flow, the right people are about to flow. You're not going to have to find them; they're going to find you. The medical report may not look good, you feel stuck in your health, but receive this into your spirit: Healing is flowing, strength is flowing, restoration is flowing, freedom is flowing. You can't get ahead in your career; people have held you down and left you out. Stay encouraged,

> *Receive this into your spirit: Healing is flowing, strength is flowing, restoration is flowing, freedom is flowing.*

for the flow is coming; promotion is going to flow, creativity is about to flow, ideas are going to flow.

I believe that every power that has stopped your flow is being broken right now. You're coming into supernatural increase, supernatural provision, supernatural healing, supernatural connections. You've heard the saying "It's showtime." God is saying, "It's flowtime." He's going to open the windows of Heaven and pour out blessings you cannot contain. One touch of His favor and you'll go from famine to flourishing, from barely enough to more than enough. Now do your part and get in agreement with Him. "Father, thank You that my job is not my source, but You are my Source. I'm grateful for this medicine, but You are my healer. I don't see how I can accomplish my dreams, but I know You have a way where I don't see a way."

I know a couple who wanted to buy a house in another state. They were looking in a certain neighborhood at a house they really liked, but every time they tried to move forward they just didn't feel good about it. After several months they found a large piece of property right on the outskirts of the subdivision. In the natural, being in the neighborhood would have been a better investment. The property values were higher. Even though they could have afforded that house, because they didn't feel peace, they purchased the other property outside the neighborhood.

Six months later two men showed up at their door. They were geologists. They told the couple they had been studying the area for several years and had discovered a massive amount of oil under the subdivision but the property was too small. There was no place for them to drill. They said, "If you'll let us lease part of your property, we'll not only give you the commission from your property, but we'll give you a commission from all the homes in the subdivision." There were twelve hundred homes in that neighborhood. Isaiah said, "God knows where the hidden riches are found." You know why? He's the One who put them there. He's the Source, the Creator, the Most High God. Nothing may be flowing now, but the Source knows where all the treasures are. He knows how to have you at the right place at the right time. He may not cause you to strike oil, but He can give you one idea that will catapult you to a new level. As He did for us when we were acquiring the Compaq Center, He can cause one person to come across your path who will help you accomplish a dream that seems impossible. He not only knows what you need, but He knows when you're going to need it.

Call on the Source

In 1997, I was walking through the church lobby before a service one Sunday morning. A man stopped me and said his cousin had a construction permit for the last full-power television station in Houston. We bought the permit and put the station on the air. I'd thought that's what I would do with my life. I loved television production, cameras, and editing. Having a station seemed like a perfect fit. Two years later, my father went to be with the Lord. I never dreamed I was going to become the pastor. Now my focus had changed. When we got the Compaq Center in 2003, we needed $100 million to renovate it, so we decided to sell the station. When we listed it for a certain price, all the experts said we'd never get that much. One man who had sold more stations than anyone in the United States said we were wasting our time asking that amount. One year later, we sold the station for more than we were asking, which was over five times what we purchased it for. Those funds were instrumental in enabling us to renovate our building.

God has already lined up everything you're going to need in the future. He's the Source. The Scripture says, "No good thing will He withhold because you walk uprightly." He knows where all the good things are. He's not going to withhold the finances, the health, the ideas, or the connections. Quit worrying about how it's going to work out.

"What if I don't have the funds, what if I can't find anyone to help me or if the medical report is not good." God is in control. He has unlimited resources. He knows how to get you to your destiny. Maybe you've tried to do this only on your own strength. You've given it your best effort and tried to get people to help you. Now it's time to go to God. Go to the Source and say, "God, I can't do this on my own. I'm asking You to turn this child around, bring this dream to pass, free me from this addiction, help me have this baby."

The Scripture says, "Call on the name of the Lord and He will answer you." Sometimes we call on people, call on our friends, or call on our spouse, but they can only do so much. When you call on the Source, the Creator of the universe, that's when things happen that you can't make happen.

> *Call on the name of the Lord and He will answer you.*

God wants us to depend on Him. We need to recognize that we can't do it on our own strength, that we are limited and have restrictions. By ourselves we'll get stuck, but when we ask God to help us, when we turn to our Creator, supernatural things happen. He is unlimited. He controls the universe. The good news is, God wants to help you. He wants to heal you, to free you, to increase you, to take you places that you've never dreamed of. He's longing to be good to you. Look to Him as your Source.

It's Already Prepared

In John 21, Peter was out fishing with some of the other disciples. Jesus had been crucified and had just risen from the dead. You can imagine how discouraged and confused Peter was now that Jesus was gone. Peter went back to doing what he knew how to do, and that was to fish. He had done this his whole life. They fished all night and caught nothing. Now he was even more frustrated. Early the next morning Jesus appeared to them. He came walking on the beach and called out to them, "Have you caught anything?" They said no. He said, "Put down your net on the right side of the boat and you'll catch some fish." When they did, they caught a whole net full of fish. Instantly Peter recognized it was Jesus speaking to them, and he jumped out of the boat and swam to the shore. Jesus had fish cooking on a fire, and He gave Peter some to eat. What Peter was trying to catch, Jesus not only had waiting for him, but He had it cooked and ready to eat. God is saying, "What you're trying to find, what you're trying to accomplish, if you'll look to Me, if you'll recognize that I'm the Source, then you'll see I have it already cooked and prepared. I have it already waiting for you."

As with Peter, we may have done something in the past and we were good at it, but there are times when God will not let what worked in the past continue to work because we'll think we're doing it through our own efforts, our own ability. He wants us to depend on Him. He wants us to see Him as the Source, to recognize His goodness. Too often we're striving to make things happen, discouraged because it's taking too long, trying to beat down doors. God is saying, "Come to Me, ask Me for help, call on My Name, acknowledge Me every day as your source." Peter worked all night trying to catch fish while Jesus was sitting on the shore with a fish dinner waiting for him. What you're believing for, God has already prepared.

The fish is already caught, the spouse is already picked out, the dream is already lined up, the healing has already been purchased. The fire is lit, the fish is on the grill, and you're about to come into a prepared blessing. God knows where all the fish are. What you couldn't do on your own strength, God is going to make happen. The fish are going to find you. Now do your part and recognize Him as your source. Every morning, say, "Father, thank You that You are my provider. You're the Source of everything good in my life. I recognize that every good thing comes from You, my Father in heaven." If you do this, I believe and declare that God is about to bring you some cooked fish, some prepared blessings. You're going to walk into favor that you've never seen, into opportunity, healing, abundance, and new levels of your destiny.

CHAPTER SIX

A Public Display

What God is going to do in your life is not just going to be done in private, where nobody sees it hidden in the background. God is going to do something in public. He's going to show out to where you not only see His power, but people around you see His power. It's one thing when God does something in secret. He turns a problem around, and nobody knows about it, showing you favor in private. But when God brings you out in public, it's a different story. When people are trying to discredit you, push you down, God opens a door you couldn't open, promotes you when you didn't have the qualifications, puts you in a position of influence. When He gives you a public display, you don't have to answer your critics; God does.

When it looked as though you had reached your limits, relatives laughed. When you told them you were going to pay off your house, they shook their heads, thinking you're kind of far out. But when you come into an explosive blessing that catapults you ahead, they won't be shaking their heads in disapproval. They'll be shaking their heads in amazement. God is going to show out not only to take you into your destiny but to prove to other people that the Lord is on your side. What He's about to do in your life publicly is not going to leave any doubt. It's one thing to *say* the Lord is on your side, and it's another to *see* the Lord is on your side. You've been saying it. You've been faithful, believing and expecting. Get ready. You're about to see it. God is going to do something so big, so unusual, that there won't be any doubt to you and to people around you that His favor is on your life.

Awesome Displays of Power

God said to the Israelites in Exodus, "I will perform wonders never done before. All the people around you will see the awesome power I display through you." God is about to display His awesome power through you. He could display it through anything—through nature, through creation, through the weather. But He says, "I'm going to display it through you." He's about to do something unprecedented, something that causes you to stand out, where there's no explanation other than Him. That sickness should've been the end. The medical report said you were done, but you defied the odds. You overcame it. God displayed His awesome power. Or some of the people you grew up with who are still struggling, can't get ahead, and are living in dys-

function. They will look at you, so
blessed, prosperous, living at a different level. Or maybe you weren't
the most qualified, you didn't have
the experience, but your business
took off. You didn't have to find
clients; they found you. That's God
displaying His awesome power. *Awe-
some* means it's not going to be ordinary, it's going to be
unusual—not natural, but supernatural.

> Awesome *means
> it's not going to be
> ordinary, it's going
> to be unusual—
> not natural, but
> supernatural.*

That's what our church building is, the former Compaq
Center—an awesome display of God's power. We were up
against opponents that were bigger, stronger, and had more
resources. Critics laughed, people made fun of us and said
we were wasting our time. But sometimes God will let you
get into a situation where there's no possible way out, so
when He turns it around everyone will know it was Him.
There won't be any doubt it was the hand of God.

Now your situation may seem impossible. There's no way
you can accomplish your dream, no way you'll get well, no
way you can pay off your house because you're so in debt.
It's a setup. God is about to display His awesome power,
not just so you can see it but so other people can see it.
David said, "God prepares a table before me in the presence of my enemies." That's not private, not hidden. God is
going to show out so your enemies—the opposition and the
critics—will all see you promoted, honored, in a position of
influence, in a public display. That's why you don't have to

prove to people who you are. You don't have to try to convince them to like you. You don't have to waste your time worried about people who are not for you. Keep running your race, honoring God, and at some point He's going to show out in such a way that your critics can't deny the favor on you. They may not like you, but they will respect you.

Every time the people who didn't want us to have our building drive by on the freeway, they may not like that we have it, but they can't deny the Lord was on our side. God has some of these public displays for you—not a secret sign, not in private. He's going to show out to prove to people who you are.

It Won't Be Done in Secret

David says in Psalm 86, "God, make a show of how much You love me so that bullies who hate me will stand there slack-jawed." That means "in astonishment." David knew what it was like to have opposition—people slandering him, people who didn't believe in him. His brothers made fun of him and his father discounted him. When he told King Saul he wanted to fight Goliath, Saul thought he was kidding. David was a teenager and didn't have any military training. When Goliath saw David and how small he was, he thought it was a joke. What's interesting is that David could have defeated Goliath in private. They could have fought alone, in a deserted part of a valley, with nobody around. It still would've been a great miracle, but God knows there are times when He has to bring you out in public so all your friends and your enemies—those who are for you and against you—will see firsthand the favor on your life.

When David faced Goliath, all the Philistine army was on the mountainside watching. The Israeli army was on the other side watching. King Saul was out there along with other leaders and people from the town who'd heard about this big fight. It was like the Super Bowl that everyone came out to see, with the odds set so against David that it was almost comical. Goliath stood over nine feet tall. He was their most experienced fighter, their champion. David was a teenager, with no armor and no training. When he ran out to face Goliath, all eyes were on him. He slung that rock and it hit Goliath in the forehead, knocking him to the ground unconscious. David went over, took Goliath's own sword in hand, and cut his head off. Everyone stood there in astonishment, slack-jawed. They couldn't believe what they had just seen. Instantly, David had influence, credibility, honor, and respect. Instead of making fun of him, dismissing him, now when they talked to David it was "Yes, sir. No, sir. Whatever you say, sir." Everything changed. His family never treated him the same way again. His father finally recognized the anointing on his life. Even the Philistines, the opposition who didn't like him, couldn't deny the Lord was on his side.

As with David, God has some of these times when He's going to prove to people who you are. He's going to open

doors you couldn't open, help you accomplish what you
couldn't accomplish on your own,
and help you defeat giants that are
much bigger. Everyone will see His
hand on your life. He is not going

> *Everyone will see His hand on your life.*

to do it in secret; it's going to be a public display.

Several years ago a gentleman was here in Houston for
treatment at the Texas Medical Center. He had a rare form
of cancer. The physician treating him was a specialist in
that area, very well-known in the medical field, one of the
best in the world. Even with the treatment, he'd given the
man only three years to live. This man told the doctor that
he was going to pray, and that he believed that God could
heal him. The doctor was a nice man but not a man of
faith. He smiled and said, "Unfortunately, this type of cancer
doesn't respond to prayer." This doctor had never seen anyone
recover from it, and he was respectful, seeing it only from a
scientific point of view. Several months later, the man went
back to see how the treatment was working. The doctor
came in, looked at his chart, and seemed puzzled, thinking
it was the wrong one. He went out, then came back in a
little later and showed the man the old chart, comparing it
to the new. He said, "In forty years of practice, I have never
seen this result. I don't see the cancer anymore." The doctor stood there in astonishment. He asked the man to write
down what he prayed, how long he prayed, and everything
else he'd done so it could be included in his research.

What was that? A public display. God showed His awesome power through this man, not just to heal him but so other people would see the hand of God. That doctor will never be the same. He may not be a believer yet, but a seed was planted in his heart. It's significant that David prayed, "God, make a show of how much You love me." He was releasing his faith, saying, "God, I believe You can take me where I can't go on my own." I wonder what would happen if we would start praying, "God, make a show of how much You love me. Display Your awesome power through me. Let me not only see Your goodness but use me to show other people how great You are."

A Public Sign Through You

In 1 Kings 18, there's a story about four hundred and fifty false prophets who worshipped the god Baal and came against the prophet Elijah. It didn't look like he had a chance; it was all of them against one of him. They agreed to settle their feud by having a contest. The false prophets and Elijah would each make an altar and put wood on it, and the god who started the wood on fire would be the true God. Sometimes, as with Elijah, you find yourself in a situation where you feel outnumbered. The sickness seems bigger, the opposition stronger, or the addiction too powerful. It's easy to get discouraged and shrink back. But you have to do as he did and not be intimidated by what's against you. The battle is not yours; the battle is the Lord's. God did not bring you this far to leave you. He allowed that situation so He could display His awesome power through you. Every circumstance may say, "You'll never get out of it. You'll never get well. The obstacle's too big." Stay in faith. God has your back.

It was four hundred and fifty against one, but the prophets of Baal didn't realize that Elijah had the Most High God on his side. They built their altar, put the wood on it, started praying, dancing, begging, shouting to Baal hour after hour. Everyone was watching, waiting, but nothing happened. Finally, Elijah said, "It's my turn." He put the rocks down for an altar, dug a trench around it, put the wood on top of it, then he told them to pour water on the wood—not once, not twice, but three times, even filling the trench. He wanted to make sure that when it caught fire, they would know it wasn't a coincidence; it wasn't just an act of nature, but it was the hand of God. Then Elijah prayed, "God of Abraham, Isaac, and Jacob, prove today that You are the Lord and that I am Your servant. Answer me so these people will know that You are God."

Think of the boldness that took. It's one thing to pray and believe, and God doesn't answer our prayer. We think, *That's no big deal. We'll pray again tomorrow. We'll keep believing.* Elijah didn't have this option. His life was on the line. It was, "God, either show up or I'm done." As soon as he finished praying, fire flashed down from Heaven and burned it all up. Everyone fell on their faces and cried, "Elijah, your God is the true God!"

God is going to do some things in your life where He doesn't just bring you out; He gives you a public sign. People around you may not believe yet, but when God displays His awesome power through you, when He promotes you even when others are trying to push you down, when He takes you to levels you've never dreamed of, they won't be able to deny it. They're going to know He is God. Elijah prayed, "God, prove that You are the Lord, and prove that I am Your child." Now, God doesn't have to prove anything. He's God whether we believe it or not, but sometimes He will prove to other people that you are His child.

When you face difficult situations and you feel outnumbered or the giant seems too big, if you do as Elijah did and ask big, God will show out big. If you say in humility, "God, prove that I'm Your child. Free me from this addiction. Turn my marriage around. Restore my health. Bring this dream to pass," He will prove not only to you but to people around you that you are His child and He is on your side. What's interesting is, when the fire hit the altar, it not only burned up the wood and evaporated the water, which fire is supposed to do, but the Scripture says the rocks were burned up. It was all gone. Rocks don't normally burn, but when God shows out in your life, He's going to change what looks permanent.

Maybe your child has been off course for years, you don't think you can break the addiction, you feel stuck in your career, and you have big obstacles in your path. Don't worry. God knows how to burn up the rocks. When He shows out,

the baby will be conceived, the loan will go through, your child
will fulfill his destiny, your health
will turn around. He's a supernatural
God. Get ready, He's about to burn
up some rocks. He's about to move
what looks permanent. It's not just
going to surprise you; it's going to
surprise the people around you.

> *It's not just going to surprise you; it's going to surprise the people around you.*

It's Time to Show Out

When I was growing up, I knew a man who owned a company
that moved houses. He was an unusual man, full of faith. It
seemed as though he would believe for anything. One day
he and his workers had traveled for hours moving a house
down backcountry roads, and they finally made it to their
location. When they started to unload the house, the man
realized he had forgotten to bring his main chain. Without
that chain, he couldn't finish. He was so disappointed because
they were way out in the country, a couple of hours from
the nearest town. It seemed as though he and his workers
would have to come back the next day to finish. He was
about to leave when he told the people around him that he
was going to pray. They kind of laughed and said, "What
are you going to pray about?" He said, "I'm going to pray
that God will give me a chain." Now they really laughed.
One of them said, "What do you think, that God's going

to rain down a chain from Heaven?" They were all making fun about it and laughing. He said, "I don't know, but the Scripture says you have not because you ask not, so I'm going to ask." Then he said, "Lord, You can do anything. You control the universe. I'm asking You to give me a chain so we don't have to waste a day and come back tomorrow." They were standing on the side of the country road, and there was a big curve right in front of them. About that time an old pickup truck came speeding down the road with its tailgate down. When it took that turn going way too fast, a chain flew out of the back of the pickup bed, slid across the road, and ended up stopping right at the man's feet. He picked it up and said, "I got my chain, men. Let's go to work."

Sometimes God will show out in your life not so much for your sake but to show other people that the Lord is on your side. Those men stood there in astonishment. When he prayed after that, they listened rather than made fun. Where are the people who will do as this man and believe God wants to display awesome power through them? Where are the people who believe God wants to make them an example of His goodness? It's good to read about God's power, it's good to talk about it, it's good to remember it, but God wants you to experience it. He wants to show out in your life in a new way. When you do as David did and pray, "God, make a show of Your favor," that's when God will make things happen that not only amaze you but amaze the people around you.

A lady I know and a friend of hers were on the same flight when the friend became ill. Her heart started racing, her blood pressure went up, and she thought she was going to pass out. This lady was away from her seat when she heard about it and rushed back to her friend and knelt down beside her in the aisle and started praying for her. With all the commotion, everyone was watching. As she prayed, the friend's heart rate began to go back down, and the dizziness began to go away. The man in the seat behind them was so impressed that he said to the lady, "What was it about your prayer that did that?" Before she could answer, turbulence suddenly hit the plane, which started going up and down, and everybody was holding on for dear life. That made the friend's heart start racing again. This lady prayed, "Lord, let these winds calm down." Right when she said it, the plane stopped shaking and went back to normal. All the turbulence stopped. That man's eyes got big. He said, "Lady, where did you get this kind of power?" She said, "It's not me; it's my God." When you believe that God wants to show out in your life and you have the boldness to ask, God will display awesome power through you and other people will notice.

> *It's not me; it's my God.*

In the book of Daniel, three Hebrew teenagers wouldn't bow to King Nebuchadnezzar's golden idol. The king was so furious that he had them thrown into a fiery furnace. When the guards opened the furnace door, it was so hot that they were instantly killed as they pushed the young men into the blaze. Those teenagers should have perished instantly, but after a few minutes the king looked into the furnace and saw not only three people but four, and the fourth one looked like the son of God. It was a great miracle that they weren't hurt, but that's not the only reason God did it. It was so other people would be changed. He's going to display power through you so people around you will know He is God. After the teenagers came out unharmed, King Nebuchadnezzar said, "Praise be to the God of Shadrach, Meshach, and Abednego." Just a few hours earlier he hadn't believed in their God. He was against them and everything they stood for. Now he was giving God praise. Why? God displayed awesome power through those teenagers.

That's what God is going to do for you. He's going to open doors you can't open, thrust you to new levels, cause you to overcome what looks impossible. The king went on to issue a decree that said, "If anyone speaks against the God of Shadrach, Meshach, and Abednego, they will be destroyed, for no God can save like their God." Words don't always affect people. You can try to convince them, debate with them. But when they see you go to levels you couldn't reach on your own, when they see you come out of the fiery furnace, beat the cancer, or break the addiction, when they see the chain curling up at your feet, opportunities chasing you down, they will know the Lord is on your side. As with Nebuchadnezzar, they will want what you have. God is not going to do this all in private. He's going to give you a public sign, something so amazing that people notice.

People Will See and Know

Before Paul became the apostle who wrote almost half the books of the New Testament, his name was Saul. He was the greatest enemy of the church. He had believers arrested and put in prison. But on the road to Damascus a bright light from Heaven flashed around him. He fell to the ground, and in that moment God revealed Himself to Saul and he became a believer. It was big news, a complete turnaround. Saul's name was eventually changed to Paul, and he saw amazing things happen in his life. One time he'd been shipwrecked and was on an island beach. When he went to pick up firewood, a poisonous snake bit his hand. He just shook it off, went about his business, and it never affected him even though the islanders saw it and said he should've swollen up and died. Another time, Paul and Silas were singing praises in prison, in the deepest dungeon at midnight, when there was a great earthquake and the prison doors flung open. The chains fell off their feet, and they could have walked out as free men. When the jailer, the one in charge of making sure they didn't escape, realized what had happened, he was so amazed that he asked them, "What must I do to be saved?"

Paul's life was full of these miracles and awesome displays of God's power. In Acts 26, he had been arrested and brought to the city of Caesarea. At trial, he defended himself before the Roman governor Festus, King Agrippa, and high-ranking military officers. As Paul told them about the events of his life and what had brought him there, he said, "I'm sure these events are familiar to you because they were not done in a corner."

What God is about to do in your life is not going to be done in a corner, hidden where nobody notices. People are going to see the favor, see the protection, the promotion, the abundance. Some people think you've reached your limits, that you'll never get out of that problem, never get well, that you don't have the talent. They're going to see God take you to levels you've never dreamed of. They're going to see you accomplish goals bigger than you've imagined. It's not only going to amaze you, it's going to amaze them. It's not going to happen in a corner. God is not going to do it in private. It's going to be a public display.

You may have some obstacles in your path, and you may feel like you're stuck. It's a setup. God allowed that so He can show out in your life. He's about to do something unprecedented. Get ready for new ground. Get ready to go where you couldn't go on your own. Every morning, get up and say as David did, "God, make a show of how much You love me." If you do this, I believe and declare that God is about to display His awesome power through you. New doors are going to open—new opportunities, healing, favor, breakthroughs. People are going to know the Lord is on your side.

CHAPTER SEVEN

Favor in the Storm

When we think of favor, we think of something good happening. We received a promotion. We met someone special. The medical report turned around. We know that's the favor of God. But when we face difficulties—things aren't going our way, we're still taking the medical treatment, our finances haven't turned around, or the promotion didn't go through—it doesn't seem as though we have favor. We have all these obstacles, but having favor doesn't mean you won't have challenges. Favor is what's keeping those challenges from defeating you. When you're in a difficult time, you may not see it, but favor is what's pushing back forces of darkness. Favor is what's keeping that sickness from taking your life. Favor is what protected you in that accident. If you didn't have favor, you wouldn't still be here. The enemy would've taken you out.

You may not recognize it, but you have favor in the storm, favor taking the treatment, favor dealing with an addiction. The Scripture says that God's favor surrounds you.

It doesn't come and go. It's with you in the good times and in the tough times.

Walking Between Walls of Water

When the Israelites left Egypt and were headed to the Promised Land, they came to the Red Sea. Pharaoh had just let them go, but then he changed his mind and he and his army came chasing them. The Israelites were at a dead end. They had nowhere to go. Moses held up his staff and the waters parted. Those two million people began to walk through on dry ground.

We look at it today and, in hindsight, it's easy to see they had favor. The waters miraculously parted. But imagine being there, having to walk between walls of water, not knowing if, at any moment, they were going to collapse. Imagine holding your children tightly, with the enemy chasing you and closing in. It was loud and chaotic. People were panicking, with all kinds of commotion surrounding them. I don't think they walked through the parted waters calmly and collectedly. They were afraid, thinking of everything that could go wrong. "What if these walls of water don't hold up, and we all drown? What if we don't make it through in time? What if Pharaoh catches us?" There were a thousand things they could have worried about. It wasn't until they got to the other side, until they were back on land and the walls of water swept over their enemies, that they began to rejoice. Then they knew they had favor. The truth is, they had favor the whole time; they just couldn't see it. Favor is what was holding back the walls of water. Favor is what kept the enemy from catching them.

When we're in the middle of a difficulty, sometimes we don't recognize that we have favor. It's easy to focus on all the negative things that could happen. "What if I don't get well? What if I can't find another job? What if my child doesn't get back on course?" You could live worried, losing sleep, panicked. No, stay in peace. You have favor in the storm. God is pushing back forces of darkness for you. He's not allowing the sickness, the addiction, or the trouble at work to keep you from your purpose. There is a force working for you in the middle of the storm that is greater than any force that's trying to stop you.

> *There is a force working for you in the middle of the storm that is greater than any force that's trying to stop you.*

When you look around, you may see walls of water. You see opposition, trouble, sickness. It looks frightening, but keep the right perspective. It cannot defeat you. As with the Israelites, the favor God put on your life is going to bring you safely through. The enemy doesn't have the final say. God does, and what He has purposed for your life will come to pass. No bad break can stop you, no sickness, no addiction, no person. God is in control. Instead of being frustrated by the problem, worried about your health, upset over the bad break, turn it around. "Father, thank You that

I have favor in the storm. Thank You that favor is keeping my enemies from defeating me."

Favor Brings You Out of the Storm

It's easy to believe we have favor when good things are happening. What I want us to see is that we have favor when we're in between walls of water. We have favor when enemies are chasing us. Sometimes we're so focused on the threat and what's coming against us that we don't recognize that, without the goodness of God, we wouldn't still be standing. The psalmist said, "God has anointed you. He is steadying you, making you strong, and your enemies will not get the best of you." In the middle of that difficulty, you need to remind yourself of who you are. You are anointed. You've been handpicked by God. He's crowned you with favor. He always causes you to triumph. Right now, He's steadying you. He's making you stronger. If you could see behind the scenes, you would see Him pushing back the opposition. You would see Him making your crooked places straight, lining up the right people to help you. Instead of complaining about the storm, you need to tell the enemy, "You are not going to get the best of me. You are messing with the wrong person. You may knock me down, but you can't knock me out. When you come against me one way, God said He will defeat you and cause you to flee seven ways."

You don't have to live worried, focused on the problems,

wondering why it happened. You know a secret. You have favor in the storm. You know God is fighting your battles. You know that what was meant for harm, He's turning to your advantage, and here's the key: The enemy wouldn't be fighting you if you weren't a threat. He wouldn't be trying to stop you if you weren't on the verge of something amazing. He knows you're about to step into a new level. He knows you're about to take new ground for your family. You're about to come into your Promised Land. You're about to see something you've never seen. The enemy can sense God is about to exceed your expectations, so he's working overtime to try to get you worried, frustrated, overwhelmed by problems, not expecting anything good. No, get ready. Favor is about to turn things around. Favor is about to catapult you to a new level. Favor is going to help you break that addiction.

"Well, Joel, if I had favor, why did I have these problems in the first place?" Favor is not going to keep you from the storm, but favor will bring you out of the storm. God wouldn't have allowed it if He didn't have a purpose for your good. We don't understand everything that happens. Sometimes life is not fair, but you have to trust that God knows what He's doing.

You Will See It No More

Before the Red Sea parted, the Israelites could have thought, *God, You said we were going to the Promised Land. You brought us out of slavery. Why did You change Your mind? Why are You going to let Pharaoh and his men recapture us?* It didn't make sense to them, but God's ways are not our ways. When that water parted, the Israelites went through on dry ground. But when Pharaoh and his army came chasing them, the waters closed back up and they all drowned.

Sometimes God will take you through a difficulty to get rid of what's chasing you. You'll make it through the storm, but what you didn't need, what was going to hinder you for years to come—the addiction, the dysfunction, the toxic relationship—won't make it through. If those enemies had not drowned, the Israelites would have lived with the constant threat that Pharaoh and his men could show up at any moment and try to recapture them. So, yes, it was nerve-racking to go through walls of water, and I'm sure they didn't like being chased by enemies, but God had a purpose.

You may not like the difficulty. It may not seem fair, but you're going to come out of that storm free from things that would have held you back your whole life. God told the Israelites, "The enemies you see today, you will see no more." God is saying that to you. That addiction that's held you back for years is not permanent. When you come through the storm, you will see it no more. That sickness, that trouble at work, the loneliness is not your destiny. Breakthroughs are coming. Freedom is coming. Healing is coming. Abundance is coming.

What's trying to stop you is only temporary. Don't be discouraged by the storm. God has you in the palms of His hands. He didn't send you into the storm by yourself. He's right there with you. The enemy cannot take you out. God has a hedge of protec-

> *God has you in the palms of His hands.*

tion around you. He controls the walls of water. It may seem frightening, but He's pushing back the opposition. As with the three Hebrew teenagers who were thrown into the fiery furnace in the book of Daniel, whom I mentioned in the previous chapter, God is the fourth man in the fire. You're not in there alone. Favor is in the fire with you.

When those teenagers came out of the furnace unharmed, without the smell of smoke, all their enemies had a new perspective. They knew there was something special about them. They knew they were anointed. The king even said, "From now on, we're going to worship their God." They didn't like going through the furnace, but God used that difficulty to get rid of what would have hindered them for their whole life. God changed their enemy's mind and gave them a new respect, and what you're going through may not be all about you. It's about God getting rid of what's hindering you. He's putting you in position to reach the fullness of your destiny.

Favor in the Famine

The Scripture says, "Do not be intimidated by your enemies." Don't be intimidated by that cancer. It's no match for our

God. He created your body. Don't be intimidated by the financial setback. Not having enough, lack, and struggle are not your destiny. You keep honoring God, being your best. You will come to a point where you see that no more. There is favor on your life that will cause you to prosper even in a desert. You will flourish even in a famine. You don't have to get out of the difficulty to succeed. You don't have to change jobs, change neighborhoods, or change positions. You have favor in the famine. God will cause you to succeed in the middle of the trouble.

This is what happened with Isaac. In Genesis 26, there was a great famine in the land. Isaac was going to move away to a different country to get out of the famine and find someplace where he could plant his crops, have good soil and plenty of water. But God told him to stay where he was, to not leave that place, and God would bless him and his descendants. God was saying, "Isaac, you don't have to go somewhere else to try to find favor. You have favor in the famine. I'm going to bless you. I'm going to prosper you in spite of what the conditions look like." Logically, it didn't make sense. The ground was hard and dry; there wasn't enough water to irrigate his crops. Isaac could have talked himself out of it, but he understood this principle that he had favor in the famine. He went out in the middle of the drought and planted his whole field. I can hear his neighbors, the Philistines, saying, "What is this guy thinking? He is wasting his time and all that good seed. Doesn't he know that nothing can grow in a famine?" Nevertheless, the Scripture says, "That year

Isaac's crops were tremendous. He harvested one hundred times more than he planted, for the Lord blessed him, and he became very wealthy."

Notice, Isaac didn't have to leave to get out of the famine and go somewhere else to be blessed. He had favor in the famine. God can increase you in spite of what's going on around you. Don't complain because you don't have something you want. "Joel, if my supervisor would give me credit...if I could move out of this neighborhood...if business wasn't so slow." There is favor on your life right now to cause you to prosper. But as long as you think you have too many disadvantages, and you're waiting to get out of the famine before you'll start believing and being your best, that will limit you. Do as Isaac did. "Father, thank You that I have favor in the famine. Thank You that You're opening doors no man can shut, causing me to stand out, bringing opportunity. Thank You that whatever I touch will prosper and succeed." Your job is not your source. God is your source. He can bless you in unusual ways. He's not limited by your salary, by your training, by your experience. He has ways to increase you that you've never thought of. He can cause people to be good to you. He can bring opportunity. He can give you ideas and creativity.

The Limitation Is in Your Thinking

A man told me recently how he received an inheritance from a family member he had never met. He didn't even know they were related. They didn't have the same last name. At first he thought it was a mistake, but that one good break put him into financial overflow. He didn't see it coming. God has some unexpected blessings, things you don't see coming. "Well, Joel, I don't know any relatives like that." Neither did he, but they found him. The Scripture speaks about how, when you honor God, when you keep Him first place, His blessings will chase you down. You don't have to go after them. They will come after you.

But too often we're focused on the conditions. "I can't expect anything good. I'm in a famine." God is not limited by the conditions, by the economy, by your job, by your family, by your training. He owns it all. As with Isaac, one touch of His favor will take you and your family to a new level. The Scripture says Isaac's wealth continued to increase. He acquired large flocks of sheep and goats and great herds of cattle and had many employees. This all started when he believed that he had favor in the famine. He could have focused on the conditions and lived with a limited mind-set. "I can't plant here. I can't expect anything good. I'm in a drought." Instead he dared to believe.

Are you letting the conditions talk you out of what God put in your heart? Are you thinking that one day when you're out of the famine, when the company promotes you, when you get the training, then you'll have favor? No, you have favor right now. Favor is what gives you the advantage. Favor

Favor is what's going to catapult you to a new level.

is what's going to catapult you to a new level. Favor is going to make things happen that you didn't see coming.

A few years ago, my sister, Lisa, and her husband, Kevin, were going to sell their house. Typical houses in their neighborhood were taking anywhere from six months to two years to sell, and they couldn't purchase their new house until they sold the old one. They could have thought, *Too bad. It's going to be a long wait. We picked the wrong time to sell.* Instead, as Isaac did, they believed they had favor in the famine, and they prayed, asking God that their house would not only sell quickly, but that they would get close to their asking price. The first day it was on the market, a lady came in and said, "I'll buy it, and if you'll take it off the market, I'll pay you more than you're asking for it."

God is not limited by the conditions. He's limited by our thinking. Why don't you take the limits off Him? Quit thinking of all the reasons why you can't be blessed or accomplish your dreams, why you won't get well or meet the right person. You may not see a way, but God has a way. When you believe, all things are possible. Isaac was so blessed that the Scripture says the Philistines became jealous of him. The same people who were making fun of him for planting in the famine, the same ones who were telling him he was wasting his time, now they were upset that he was being blessed.

It's funny how people who won't do what you're willing to do will become jealous when you're blessed and they're not. You dared to take the step of faith. You dared to pray, to stretch, to plant, to believe. Now you're seeing increase and favor. Don't be surprised when the Philistines show up. The naysayers are not happy when they see you rising higher. They'll find fault, criticize, and try to bait you into conflict. Just run your race. It's not about you. It's about the favor on your life. Don't let the chatter, the negative comments, the jealousy, or the envy distract you. You don't have to answer to people. You don't have to prove yourself. Stay focused on your goals, and God will take care of the Philistines. God will take care of the opposition.

Opposition Will Promote You

In Chapter Two, I stated that a man named Zerubbabel was rebuilding the temple in Jerusalem. It had been destroyed years earlier, and the king had issued a decree to have it rebuilt. Everything was going great. He laid the foundation and built the altar. Then the opposition came, the people who didn't want it rebuilt. They started bribing the workers, paying people to cause trouble, stirring up all kinds of turmoil. Zerubbabel could have thought, *God, I'm doing what You asked me to do, but I have all this opposition. These powerful people are coming against me.* It didn't look as though he had favor. It looked as if his enemies were getting the best of him, but you can't see what God is doing behind the scenes. It may look as though it's going to stop you, but if you stay in faith, God will use it to promote you.

The people opposing the rebuilding sent a letter to their

king, lying about Zerubbabel, saying, "The people who are rebuilding the temple are evil people. They're going to try to overthrow you. They're not going to pay taxes. It's going to be a big mistake." In response, the king ordered that work on the temple be stopped, and it came to a standstill for seventeen years. Then the prophets Haggai and Zechariah urged Zerubbabel and the people to resume the work on the temple despite the order. When the governor of the region asked Zerubbabel who'd given him permission to rebuild it, he told the governor, "We are servants of the Most High God, and there was a temple built here by a great Israeli king years earlier. Your King Cyrus issued a decree to have this temple rebuilt." So the governor asked the king to search the royal archives, and they found the decree of Cyrus. Then the king issued a new decree especially directed at the opposition that said, "Do not hinder these people. Let them rebuild the temple. Not only that, but I decree that you are to help them. You are to use my funds to pay the full construction cost, and you are to take them food and supplies every day." They meant it for harm. God turned it for good.

You may have people and circumstances coming against you. God knows how to cause it to backfire. The opposition was trying to stop Zerubbabel, but they ended up having to help him. Without their opposition, he wouldn't have had the temple totally paid for. Not only that, they had to bring them food every day. God has said He'll prepare a table before you in the presence of your enemies. Sometimes He'll even have your enemies serve you dinner. I can hear Zerubbabel saying,

"Can I get some ketchup with my french fries?" God knows how to vindicate you. When people are trying to hold you down or stir up trouble, stay in peace. It's going to backfire.

> *The trap the enemy sets for you, they will fall in themselves.*

The psalmist said, "The trap the enemy sets for you, they will fall in themselves." God is working in ways that you cannot see. It may look like opposition. The truth is, it's the hand of God setting you up for promotion.

Sometimes Favor Is Hidden

When you face difficult challenges that you don't understand, that doesn't mean that somehow you've stepped out of favor or that God's forgotten about you. It's a setup. It's all a part of God's plan to take you to the next level. You may not like some of the things that are frustrating you—the people coming against you, the closed doors, the disappointments— but without them, you couldn't reach the fullness of your destiny. The man named Job in the Scriptures would never have received double if God had not allowed him to be tested, to go through adversity, unfair situations. In chapter 10 of the book of Job, he said, "I know God has granted me favor." What's interesting is that he didn't see things restored until chapter 42. Right in the middle of the difficulty, when it looked as though everything had gone wrong, instead of complaining, Job was saying, "Father, thank You that I have

Your favor." He understood this principle that he had favor in the difficulty, favor when it didn't look like it.

Sometimes favor is hidden. You can't see it in the storm, in the betrayal, in the loss. People could look at you and think, *You don't have favor. You're struggling. You're still dealing with that illness. Those people at work are holding you back.* It may look as though you're stuck, but you can't see what's happening behind the scenes. You don't know what God is up to. Months after Job went into adversity, he not only came out, but he came out with twice what he had before. What looks as if it's going to keep you from your destiny is rather going to launch you into a

> *It may look as though you're stuck, but you can't see what's happening behind the scenes.*

new level of your destiny. Those obstacles are not going to stop you. They're going to promote you.

Keep the right perspective. You don't have to live worried and panicked because you're in between walls of water. You have favor in the storm, favor in the famine. Right now, God is pushing back forces of darkness. Favor is keeping your enemies from defeating you. It may have been meant for your harm, but get ready. I believe and declare it's about to backfire. As with Zerubbabel, you're about to see what God's been doing behind the scenes. People who were against you are suddenly going to be for you. Problems are about to turn around. Unexpected blessings are coming your way, with breakthroughs, vindication, promotion, and healing.

CHAPTER EIGHT

Your Set Time for Favor

In the Old Testament, the Israelites had several different feasts that they were to observe each year. These feasts, such as Passover and the Feast of Weeks (Pentecost), were at set times based on the cycle of the moon and certain other criteria. The times had been ordained by God and couldn't be changed. These were special times that God had set aside to bless His people. He had already established when to show them favor.

Just as it was with them, there are set times God has already ordained to show out in your life. We can all look back and see these times when we got a break that we didn't deserve, things fell into place, maybe your career took off. After years of things being routine, average, you came into a season of growth, a season of increase, a season of blessing. What was that? A set time of favor.

I talked to a man recently who'd had back pain for eight years. He hurt his back playing football in college. He'd had surgery, gone through treatment, rehab, and took pain pills. Nothing seemed to help. He'd already decided he'd have to live with that pain for the rest of his life. But about six months before we talked, out of the blue things started getting better and better. He said, "Joel, I don't know what happened. The doctors can't explain it, but today I'm totally free from this pain." As with the Israelites, he came into one of his set times.

This Is a New Season

The Psalms speak about how God's favor surrounds us like a shield. It doesn't come and go. Favor is always with us, but there are set times when God's favor will show out. Set times when God will thrust you from the background to the foreground. Set times when God will accelerate your dreams and make things happen faster than you thought. Set times, as with my friend, when you'll get well even though the report says it's not going to happen, when the problem will unexpectedly turn around even though it looks impossible.

You need to get ready. I believe you've come into one of your set times of favor. Maybe you've been struggling, everything's been uphill, but you're going to see an anointing of ease. God is going before you. He's going to cause things to fall into place. At work, you've been doing your best, working hard, but not getting the credit you deserve

> *I believe you've come into one of your set times of favor.*

because coworkers are playing politics. Don't worry. In the set time God is going to promote you. He's going to push you up. He's going to set you on high. Or perhaps you've been through some relationships that didn't work out, and now you think you'll always be lonely. No, in this set time God is bringing a divine connection, somebody better than you have imagined. They're already ordained to come across your path. Now you may not see how this is going to happen. Your mind will tell you, "You'll never get well." "You'll never meet the right person, never accomplish that dream." Don't believe those lies. The Creator of the universe has already established your set times. His power is greater than any force that's trying to come against you.

Now do your part and get in agreement with God. "Lord, I believe this is my set time for favor. The medical report may not look good, but I believe it's my set time to get well." "My dream looks as though it's going to take years, but Lord, I want to thank You that it's my set time for acceleration."

You may have tried some things in the past, but it didn't work out. The business wasn't successful. The loan didn't go through. The diet didn't work. You need to try it again. This is a new season.

A man I met in the church lobby told me how he had a dream to start his own business. He got it going, everything was fine, he was so excited, but he hit a series of setbacks. Unfortunately, it didn't make it. He thought he was done, that it would never happen. No, it just wasn't the right time. Don't give up on what God promised you. Don't let that dream die stillborn. It may not have happened in the past, but you've come into a set time. God has favor waiting for you, ideas waiting for you, the right people waiting for you. Try it again.

The Scripture says, "A good man falls seven times, but the Lord raises him back up." The loan didn't go through because you didn't qualify for that new house. Try again. You're in a set time of favor. You tried to lose the weight, tried to get back in shape, but it didn't work out. Try it again. God is breathing on your life in a new way. He's given you the ability, determination, and strength to do what you couldn't before. Now all through the day, especially in the tough times, say, "Lord, thank You that it's my set time for favor. Thank You that You're helping me do what I could not do on my own."

Your Time Has Come

In Psalm 102, the psalmist was having an incredibly difficult time and began to pray. He went into great detail to list all his troubles. He said, "God, I'm sick. I'm down to skin and bones. I can't sleep at night. I've lost all my income. I'm lonely. My friends have left me. My enemies taunt me all day long. Now I'm just sitting among the ashes." For eleven verses he goes on and on, telling how miserable his life is, how he feels overwhelmed by his trouble. Just reading it can make you feel depressed. But just when you think he's about to give up, just about to throw in the towel, he says in verse twelve, "But You, O Lord, are still on the throne. For You will arise and have mercy on Zion, for the time to favor her, yes, the set time, has come." Zion is the church. You can put your name in place of Zion. "For You will arise and have mercy on Linda, for the time to favor her, yes, the set time, has come." "You will arise and have mercy on those people at Lakewood, for the time to favor them, yes, the set time, has come." In the midst of his sad song, in the midst of listing all his difficulties, deep down he knew there was a set time of favor in his future. At that point, the Israelites had been through seventy years of hardships, all kinds of struggling. God said, "Do not worry. Things are about to change."

You've come into your set time of favor. The Scripture says, "God will arise and have mercy." In this set time, God will step in against your enemies. You won't have to fight those battles; the Most High will arise. And when He arises, enemies will be scattered. When He arises, sicknesses will be defeated, addictions will be broken; lack, struggle, and poverty will come to an end. He's going before you clearing the path, pushing back the forces of darkness, making a way where you could not go before.

In this set time, the enemies you've seen in the past you will see no more. For the addictions, bad habits, things you haven't been able to overcome, this is a new day. God is arising. It's your set time for freedom, your set time for wholeness. Those obstacles in your career, when you

> *God is arising.*

can't seem to get the break you need, when you can't get over the hump—things are about to change. God is fighting your battles, causing you to stand out, bringing you from obscurity to prominence. This is a set time for God to thrust you where you could not go on your own.

Don't talk yourself out of it. You may feel as though you're in verses one through eleven of that psalm right now. As with that man, you can come up with good reasons why you won't get well, why you won't be successful. "I have a lot of powerful people coming against me." "I have this medical condition that looks permanent." "I don't have the experience, the resources, or the connections to really be successful." That may all be true, but don't stop in verse eleven. Come on down to twelve and thirteen. Dare to say, "But you, O Lord, are still on the throne. You have set this time to favor me." What God lifts up, no person can push down. What God breathes life into, sickness cannot take away. What God blesses, all the forces of darkness cannot curse. Our attitude should be, *Yes, this obstacle looks big, this sickness, this legal situation. But I know a secret: God is still on the throne, and He has set this time for me to overcome. This is my set time to break through. This is my set time to live in victory.* We should say, "God will arise."

Let me tell you, when God gets up, the enemy trembles. In your set time, God is not going to sit idly by. Yes, we all have seasons of testing and trials when we have to stand strong and prove to God that we'll be faithful. But in this set time of favor, that's when God gets up and says, "Okay, that's enough. Let Me go to work." He'll put a stop to what's trying to stop you. He's said the trap the enemy set for you, they will fall into themselves. He's said no weapon formed against you will ever prosper. Don't be intimidated. You're not weak. You're not lacking. The Most High God has risen on your behalf. He's got your back. He's got you covered. He's saying, "It's your set time for favor, your set time for healing, your set time for acceleration."

Now you have to let this seed take root inside. All through the week have this expectancy and say, "Lord, thank You that it's my set time for favor, that You're giving me power to do what I could not do before. Lord, thank You that You're causing me to stand out, drawing the right people to me, that Your blessings and favor are overtaking me." "Well, Joel, I believe maybe one day that will happen for me." No, I'm asking you to come over into the now. Today is your set time for favor—not in three months, not six years from now. God said the time to favor you has come.

The Alarm Is Going Off

The Amplified Bible says, "The moment designated has come." There are moments that God has already designated to show out in your life. I believe this is one of your moments. You're living in a favor season, a growing season, an acceleration season. You're going to have a new confidence to do things that you couldn't do before. You're going to see your gifts and talents come out in a greater way. God is going to give you more influence, more prominence, a bigger platform. His face is going to shine down on you and cause you to stand out. Things are about to change for your family members who have been off course, who seem as though they'll always make poor choices. Those forces are being broken. They're going to start making good choices that honor God. People are going to think, *How in the world did they turn around so quickly?* Here's how: You came into a set time of favor, a moment already designated by the Creator of the universe.

Think about a set time. Sometimes at night you'll set your clock or phone alarm for the morning. "I want to get up at 6:30," you say, and you set the hour, set the minute. That's the set time. Or maybe you're cooking something that takes an hour. You set the timer on the oven for sixty minutes. You're waiting and waiting. But when the alarm goes off, you don't keep waiting. The set time has come. You change your position, you change your posture. You take the food out; it's done. You wake up; the morning has arrived.

I believe that God is saying to us, "The alarm is going off. The set time has come." Change your position, change your attitude from *I don't think it's ever going to happen* to *Lord, thank You that it's here. Thank You that my set time for favor has arrived.* Start expecting God's goodness. Life can get so routine that we're not really releasing our faith. We've been lulled into thinking, *Oh, it's never going to happen for me. It's been so long. I'll never get well. I'll never meet the right person.* No, every morning when you wake up, just imagine the alarm is going off. God is saying, "It's the set time." Our attitude should be, *This is my day for favor. This is my day for increase. This is my day for divine connections.* It should not be, *Maybe one day it's going to happen.* No, you need to declare, "I know today is my day. By faith I can hear the alarm going off. It's favor time. It's healing time. It's acceleration time. It's blessing time."

> *It's favor time. It's healing time. It's acceleration time. It's blessing time.*

You probably know what "Miller Time" is. I'm talking about breakthrough time, victory time, abundance time. I've seen this set time of favor in my own life, which is why it's easy for me to encourage you. I shouldn't be where I am. I didn't train to do what I'm doing. I wasn't planning on being a minister. I never thought I could get up in front of people. When my father went to be with the Lord and I stepped up to pastor the church, we never dreamed it would grow. We thought that it would be a victory if we could maintain what my parents had built. But what we experienced is the sovereignty of God. I came into a set time of favor that the Creator of the universe had ordained for me before I was formed in my mother's womb. God had already set aside, "That's the time I'm going to show out in Joel's life." I couldn't have made it happen. I couldn't have orchestrated the purchase of the Compaq Center, or the influence, or the growth in my own strength. It was the hand of God taking me where I could not go on my own. God set the time for us to have our building. He set the time for me to meet Victoria, and He set the time for my mother to be healed from terminal cancer.

In the same way, God has already designated these moments of favor for you. He's already set the time. You're living in one of those right now—a set time of acceleration, a set time of greater influence, a set time when God wants to show out in your life. But if this is going to happen, down in your spirit you have to hear the alarm going off. Through your eyes of faith, you have to see God arising, fighting your battles, moving obstacles out of your path, preparing the way for you to step into a new level of your destiny.

Windows of Opportunity

I talked to a young lady who moved to Houston from another state. She had tried to get her business started in the Northeast, but things didn't work out, and she felt that she was supposed to take a step of faith and move here. During her thirteen-hour drive to Texas, she listened to my messages on SiriusXM and never turned it off. I'd get tired of hearing myself for thirteen hours. When she heard one message about how God can accelerate your dreams and make things happen faster than you thought, something came alive inside.

She thought, *Yes, that's for me.* She started in her new sales position, and realistically she knew it would take a while to build up a clientele and really get things going. But she said that in the first month she sold more than she sold in the whole previous year back at home. She was so excited and said, "Joel, there are still six days left in this month, and I'm going to sell even more!" What happened? She came into her set time of favor, her set time of acceleration. But I wonder what would have happened if she had thought, *I'm never going to see favor. I'm never going to see acceleration. It's going to be rough getting started in a new city.* That would have limited her destiny.

God works where there's faith. You may not see how it can happen in the natural. That's okay; He's a supernatural God. You don't have to figure it all out. All you have to do is believe. Take the limits off God. Dare to do as she did and say, "God, just as You promised in Psalm 102 that it was the set time to favor Zion,

> *You don't have to figure it all out. All you have to do is believe.*

I know that I am Zion, I am the church, so I believe it's my set time for favor, my set time for acceleration, my set time to go to a new level."

A mother called the other day and told how she has an adult child who's physically challenged, and this child recently had a stroke and needed constant care. This mother is a widow and couldn't afford to quit her job. There was a well-respected facility that takes care of disabled people not far from where she lives. But when she inquired, she was told there was a ten-year waiting list to get in. She didn't know what she was going to do. This mother wasn't raised in church, and she didn't have any spiritual background, but through watching us on television she had come to know the Lord. She heard me talking about acceleration. In her own simple way, with a childlike faith, she said, "God, they said it's going to take ten years to get my child in. But, Lord, I believe that You can make it happen sooner." Three weeks later the facility called her back and said, "We've had an opening come up unexpectedly. We'd love to have your child." What could have taken ten years, God did in a fraction of the time. A set time of favor. A moment God had already designated.

The common denominator with both of these ladies is they released their faith. They had an expectancy. If the mother of the disabled child would have thought, *Oh, great, ten years. Just my luck. What am I going to do?* maybe the door wouldn't have opened. Maybe the set time would have been delayed. Instead of being negative, talking themselves out of it, these two ladies acted as though the alarm was going off. They changed their position, changed their attitude. They even dared to ask God for what seemed impossible.

When that alarm is sounding, when it's your time, that's a window of opportunity. It's not going to last forever. Don't let the negative voices convince you that you're never going to get well, never getting out of debt, never getting your child in, that too many people are in front of you. No, in this set time, God knows how to take you from the back to the front. He can open doors that no man can shut. He'll take you where you could not go on your own.

Every Chain Broken

My father had a sister named Mary, and for years she struggled with a condition that caused her to have violent convulsions and terrible headaches. It was so bad that it crippled her life. At one point she started having hallucinations and her mind became unclear. She was in the hospital for a long time, and they finally sent her home. She couldn't recognize people or feed herself. She had to have twenty-four-hour care. My father lived in a different city, traveled a lot, and didn't realize how sick Mary was. One day his mother called and told him about Mary's condition. He was scheduled to go out of town the next morning, but while he was praying he heard God say this distinct phrase to him, not out loud but right down in his spirit: "The hour of Mary's deliverance has come." He heard what God said in Psalm 102: "The set time for Mary's healing is here." Instead of taking his planned trip, that morning he drove from Houston to Dallas, where Mary lived.

When he went into her room, it was dark. The shades were pulled. It was very depressing. Mary didn't recognize him. Her hair was matted and her eyes were glazed over. Something rose up in my father, not just a boldness but a holy anger. As the Scripture says, "In this set time, God won't sit idly by. He'll rise up against your enemies." My father could feel that power rising up through him. He went over to Mary's bed, and after he prayed for her, he said forcefully, "Mary, I want you to get up out of this bed." All of a sudden, Mary sat straight up. She had not walked in months, but at that moment she got out of the bed and was able to walk through the house. Her mind cleared, and she was able to talk with my father. That day she went to the table and fed herself. She no longer needed her medicine or the twenty-four-hour care. She was totally healed. This was a moment of favor.

My father asked her later, "Mary, why did you get out of bed so suddenly?" She said, "Because I heard God tell me to get out." He kind of laughed and said, "No, Mary, it was me. I said it." She said, "No, John. I heard the voice of God telling me to get out of bed." He said, "Mary, I was standing right there. I'm telling you that I'm the one who said it." She said, "Listen here, John, I know what I heard. And I heard the Creator of the universe, the Most High God, tell me to get out of bed. And when I heard that, every chain was broken off me and every fiber of my being came back to life."

> *When it's your set time, all the forces of darkness cannot hold you back.*

When it's your set time, all the forces of darkness cannot hold you back. Our God is more powerful than any sickness, any addiction, any depression, any person, any hater.

Every chain will be broken, every stronghold will come down, and every limitation will be loosed. The Creator of the universe will make you come alive. He'll push you into your destiny. I believe right now God is rising up against your enemies, rising up against that sickness, that legal problem, that spirit of lack and struggle. Those forces are being broken. Your destiny is being released. Psalm 102 goes on to say that in this set time of favor, people all around you are going to notice what God has done. He's going to show out in your life in such a way that you will be an example of His goodness—so blessed, so healthy, so strong, so generous, so talented. People all around you will see the hand of God is upon your life.

But sometimes when we've been waiting a long time, waiting for the miracle, waiting for the healing, waiting for a dream to come to pass, it's easy to get into a wait mode when we're not expecting anything. God is saying, "The wait is over. The alarm is going off. Victory is here. Healing is here. Favor is here. The moment designated has come." You may not see it yet, but here's the whole key: You have to walk by faith and not by sight. All through the week say, "Lord, thank You that it's my set time for favor. Thank You that You're pushing back the forces of darkness. Thank You that You're accelerating my dreams to come to pass."

"Well, I tried this, but my business didn't work out. I didn't break the addiction. The loan didn't go through." I'm asking you to try it again. This is a new day. In this set time of favor, God is not going to sit idly by. This time

He's going to arise and fight your battles. This time He said He'll get off the throne and do what you could not do. He's breathing in your direction in a new way right now. It's your time to possess the land. If you do this, I believe and declare God is going to show out in your life in a new way. You're going to see new levels of influence, prominence, a bigger platform. As with my father's sister, there's healing from what looks permanent. As with those two ladies, you're going to accomplish more in a fraction of the time. You're going to see acceleration, where God thrusts you into a new level of your destiny.

CHAPTER NINE

The God Who Crosses His Arms

God has things in store for you that you don't see coming. It may seem as though you've reached your limits, you've gone as far as you can, but God is going to open doors you never thought would open. You didn't have the training, you weren't next in line, but somehow you were chosen for the promotion. God has unexpected favor for you. He's going to do things that you didn't deserve.

That's what happened in Genesis 48. Jacob was an old man and about to die. His son Joseph was the prime minister of Egypt, second in command under Pharaoh. Joseph was Jacob's second youngest son and his favorite. He'd given Joseph his coat of many colors and was so proud of him, but for many years Jacob thought Joseph was dead. His brothers told their father that Joseph had been torn to pieces and eaten by a wild animal when in fact they had sold him into slavery. Jacob was heartbroken and lived with all this pain.

Some thirteen years later, Jacob found out that Joseph was still alive and in this position of great honor. Joseph eventually brought his father and his entire family to Egypt, gave them places to live, and took care of them. Now Jacob was 140 years old and about to pass. Joseph went in to say his good-byes and to receive the blessing from his father. He took his two sons with him, Manasseh and Ephraim. When Jacob saw the boys, he asked who they were. Joseph said, "Dad, these are my sons, your grandsons." Imagine how Jacob must have felt. He never thought he would see Joseph again. He'd already accepted that he was gone. Now God not only let him see his son, but he saw his grandsons. His heart was overjoyed.

As Jacob did, you may have given up on a dream. You think it's been too long. You've accepted that you'll never get well, never meet the right person, or never start that business. But what God put in your heart, He's not only still going to bring to pass, but it's going to turn out better than you thought. It will be not just your son, but your grandsons as well, so to speak. It's going to exceed what you're thinking.

Adopted as Sons and Daughters

Jacob called Manasseh and Ephraim over and hugged them and kissed them. He said to Joseph, "I'm adopting your two boys as my own sons. They will receive an equal share of my inheritance just as you and your brothers receive." What's interesting is that these boys were born from an

Egyptian mother. Back then, the Egyptians worshipped idols. They didn't believe in Jehovah. She didn't have a heritage of faith. You might think God would say, "I'm not going to have anything to do with those boys. I'm not going to bless someone who comes from a family that doesn't worship Me." But God doesn't disqualify you because of how you were raised. You may come from a family that didn't honor God. There might be a lot of compromise and dysfunction in your past. The good news is, that doesn't have to stop you. As Jacob did with Manasseh and Ephraim, God is adopting you in spite of what you did or didn't do.

You may feel as though you've been under a generational curse because of how you were raised. God is choosing you to start a generational blessing. You're the difference maker. You can be the one to affect your family line for generations to come. It was extremely significant that these boys were adopted by Jacob. Not only did he overlook who their mother was, but they were grandsons, not sons. They should have had to wait another generation, forty years, to receive what Jacob was giving them. Normally their inheritance would have come from their father, Joseph. He would have passed down the blessing, the inheritance that was given to him. These boys were receiving something that they didn't deserve. This was showing us the character of God.

> *You're the difference maker. You can be the one to affect your family line for generations to come.*

There are things that we don't deserve. We were off course, doing our own thing, but God, who is full of mercy, said, "I'm going to reach down in spite of your past, in spite of your mistakes, in spite of what your family didn't do, and I'm going to adopt you anyway." Paul wrote in Ephesians that God has adopted us into His own family. Because you've been adopted, you're going to come into blessings that you didn't earn and favor that you didn't deserve. The Scripture says, "You're going to come into houses that you didn't build and vineyards that you didn't plant." Your past is not going to limit you. How you were raised is not going to keep God from blessing you.

As with these boys' mother, there may have been people in your family who didn't honor God, didn't make good choices. God is not holding that against you. He's saying, "I'm adopting you anyway, and not as My grandchild, not as My great-grandchild. I'm adopting you as My own son, My own daughter." Joseph's sons shouldn't have been heirs for another generation, but because of what Jacob did, they were thrust forty years up the road. There are things that should take you years to accomplish—years to get out of debt, years to break an addiction, years to set a new standard—but God is going to do for you what Jacob did for those boys. He's going to catapult you ahead. You're going to see things happen faster than you thought. It should have taken you a generation, but God's going to do a quick work. Because you're honoring Him, because you say, "As for me and my house, we will serve the Lord," God is speeding things up.

What should have taken your whole life is going to happen in a fraction of the time.

I can imagine that when Joseph's brothers saw the two grandsons getting the same blessing that belonged to them they didn't understand it. They said, "Dad, that's not fair. We're sons, not grandsons. You're giving them the same thing that you're giving us." Can I tell you that favor is not fair? It's just the goodness of God, and when God blesses you, don't be surprised if some people get jealous. Some people won't understand why God speeds things up for you, breaks down barriers for you. They'll start saying that you don't deserve it, you're not talented, you're just lucky. It's not luck. It's favor. It's God shining down on you, making things happen that you could not make happen.

Now stay on the high road. You don't have to convince people to like you. Some people can't handle your success, and if they walk away, let them walk. You don't need them. If they leave you, they're not a part of your destiny. Don't waste your valuable time with people who won't celebrate the blessing that God put on your life. Don't apologize for it. Don't try to downplay it. You didn't choose it. God chose you. You were a grandson. He is the One who said, "I'm adopting you. I'm giving you what you don't deserve. I'm taking you to a new level." Wear your blessings well. It's the favor of God on your life.

> *Wear your blessings well.*

Receive the Double Portion

After Jacob told his grandsons that he was adopting them, he called them over to give them his blessing. In the Old Testament, the blessing from the father was very significant and very revered. What the father spoke over the sons in his final days carried great weight and would affect the children for the rest of their lives. The oldest son would receive a double portion. That was the tradition. The blessing the father gave with his right hand was this double-portion blessing, so Joseph brought his firstborn son, Manasseh, and placed him at his father's right side so Jacob could easily reach out and touch him. Ephraim, the younger son, stood on his left. Joseph knelt down and put his face toward the ground, but Jacob, instead of reaching out with his right hand and touching Manasseh, crossed his arms and put his right hand on Ephraim and his left on Manasseh. Then he spoke the blessing over them.

When Joseph eventually looked up and saw the crossed arms, he was upset. He got up in a hurry and said, "Dad, what are you doing? You've got it backward. Manasseh is my oldest." He took Jacob's right hand and was going to place it on Manasseh, but Jacob pulled it back. He said, "I know what I'm doing. Manasseh will be great, but Ephraim will be even greater. Multitudes of nations will come out of him." God was showing us that He doesn't always bless the way we expect. Ephraim wasn't next in line. He didn't deserve it. He wasn't born in the right position, but God bypassed the tradition. He bypassed what people thought would happen and did something out of the ordinary. When Joseph tried to stop his father, Jacob said, in effect, "I know Ephraim was born second, and I know this doesn't belong to him, but I'm crossing my arms on purpose. I'm going to show him favor that he doesn't deserve."

This story is not so much about one family member getting ahead of another. It's God showing us how He can take people from the back, people who don't have the position, people who feel left out, and bring them to the front. God loves to choose people whom others say are not qualified. They don't have the talent. They don't come from the right family. They've made too many mistakes. Don't believe those lies. God is about to cross His arms. He's going to put you in a position that you didn't earn. You didn't qualify for it. You weren't next in line. God is going to make things happen that you didn't see coming.

You may think, as I once did, that where you are now is where you're always going to be. You've reached your limits. That would all be true except for one thing: God is going to cross His arms. You keep honoring God, being your best. He will open doors you never dreamed would open. He's going to promote you even though you aren't next in line. You'll think, *How did I get here? I didn't have the training,*

> *You keep honoring God, being your best. He will open doors you never dreamed would open.*

the experience, or the connections. Here's how: God crossed His arms.

I think, *How did I end up in front of so many people?* Nineteen years ago, I was running the television cameras and doing the production. I wasn't next in line necessarily, and I wasn't the most qualified. But God crossed His arms, and here I am. How did we get the Compaq Center? We weren't the most influential group in the bidding process. We didn't have the biggest portfolio or the most resources, but God crossed His arms. He took us from the back and put us in the front. How is my mother still alive thirty-eight years after being diagnosed with terminal cancer? God crossed His arms. He did what medicine could not do.

From the Back to the Front

We can all come up with excuses to settle where we are. "I don't have the training, Joel. I don't have the connections, the confidence, the talent, the size, the personality." God says, "I know all that. I created you. I know what order you were born in." You may not be the firstborn son, so to speak. You don't feel as though you have what you need to go further. Don't worry. God's going to cross His arms. He's going to make things happen that you can't make happen.

In the Scripture, Gideon said, "God, I can't lead the people of Israel against the Midianites. I come from the poorest family. I'm the least one in my father's house." God said,

"Gideon, I know you're not qualified, and I know you're not next in line, but I'm going to cross My arms. I'm going to take you from the background to the foreground. I'm going to give you influence and ability that you've never had."

When Samson was being held in prison by the Philistines, he could have said, "God, I don't deserve Your goodness. You gave me supernatural strength, and I blew it. I kept giving in to temptation. Now I'm blind, bound, grinding at the mill, and it's all my own fault." God said, "Samson, I knew every mistake you would ever make, and My mercy is bigger than anything you've done wrong. Yes, you should die defeated, feeling like a failure, but take heart. I'm going to cross My arms." God blessed Samson with supernatural strength one more time, and he defeated more enemies in his death than he did during his whole lifetime. You may have a thousand reasons why you can't accomplish your dream, why you can't get out of that problem. God is saying to you, "I'm about to cross My arms. I'm going to show you unexpected favor, unexpected promotion, unexpected healing, unexpected breakthroughs." You didn't see it coming. You aren't qualified. You weren't the next in line. It's just the goodness of God.

"Well, Joel, this is encouraging, but I don't know. I have some big problems. I have a lot coming against me." The Scripture says, "Is the arm of the Lord too short to deliver you?" Do you think that somehow God's arm can't reach you, that you're too far back, that you've made too many mistakes, missed too many opportunities, and have too big of a problem? Can I tell you that God's arm is not too short to deliver you, to heal you, to provide for you, to free you, to vindicate you? You're going to see God do things that you didn't see coming. When He crosses His arms, things are going to fall into place. Good breaks are going to find you. Opportunity is going to chase you down.

A man I know owns a design company. He started with three small clients when his main competitor already had thousands of clients. Even though he was just a speck compared to them, some of the people at the other company were jealous of his work, and they would make disparaging remarks and try to belittle him. He didn't pay any attention to it. He kept running his race, being his best. One client led to another. He kept growing. New doors kept opening. Eventually he grew to the place where he passed up that other company. One day they called and asked if he would like to purchase them. Today he owns the company that used to be hundreds of times bigger than his. He told me, "Joel, I didn't see this coming. I never dreamed I would be this successful." Now the people who used to make fun of him no longer call him bad names. Do you know what they call him? *Boss.* What happened? God crossed His arms. You may not have the position yet, the influence, the reputation, or the confidence. You feel as though you're further back. That's okay. Just keep honoring God and you will come into this unexpected favor, this promotion that you didn't see coming.

The Decision Has Been Made

In the book of Luke, the angel said, "Mary, the Lord has decided to bless you." There are some blessings that come from being faithful and doing the right thing when it's hard. But there are times, as with Mary, as with Ephraim, when God has simply decided to bless you. You didn't do anything to earn it. In fact, there were plenty of reasons why it shouldn't have happened. Maybe you didn't make good choices or you had a family member, such as Ephraim's mother, whose background didn't honor God, but God, in His mercy, crossed His arms. He chose to be good to you. He chose to turn that problem around that you got yourself into. He chose to open that door that you never could have opened. That's God deciding to bless you.

He chose to be good to you.

This is what happened with my father. He was raised in a good family, but they didn't have any kind of faith. You would think that when God needed a pastor, when He needed somebody to carry out His will, He would have found somebody from a family of faith, but God doesn't always choose who we would choose. At seventeen years of age, my father was walking home from a nightclub at two o'clock in the morning as he'd done many times before, but this time there was something different. For some reason he looked up at the stars and began to think about God. He wondered what he would do with the rest of his life. His family was very poor. They were cotton farmers. He thought he'd have to pick cotton the rest of his life. It was all he knew how to do, but as he looked up at those stars, deep down he knew he was made for more. He didn't understand anything about God, but that night he felt something special.

When he got home, he noticed the family Bible on the coffee table. It was there as a decoration. Something told him to open it. When he did, it fell open to a painting of Jesus standing at a door and knocking. The caption read: "I stand at the door and knock. If you open it, I will come in." My father didn't understand theology, but he understood opening a door. The next day he went to church with a friend for the first time. At the end of the service, the pastor invited people to come to the front who wanted to receive Christ. My father wanted to go, but he was too nervous. He wouldn't budge. His friend turned and said, "John, if you'll go, I'll go with you." They walked down to the front together. My father gave his life to Christ, the first one in our family.

But I think, *Why my father? Why did he feel that pull? Why did he look up at the stars and begin to think about his destiny? Why did the Bible fall open to a painting he could understand? Why did that friend take an interest and walk down the aisle with him?* That was the Lord deciding to bless my father, and the Lord deciding to be good to my family. My father wasn't next in line to become a pastor. He wasn't qualified. He didn't come from the "right family." Can I tell you, none of that matters? When God decides to bless you,

He'll show you favor that you didn't earn, mercy that you didn't deserve. It wasn't anything you did. It was just God crossing His arms. Where would I be if God had not decided to be good to my father? Where would my children be if God had not crossed His arms? My father not only went on to become a great pastor, found Lakewood, and touch the world, but Daddy broke the curse of poverty that he was raised in. He set a new standard for our family.

I believe that as God did for my father, as He's done for me, God has decided to bless you. He's decided to bring your family in. He's decided to take you to new levels. Circumstances may say it's not going to happen, you're not qualified, you're not next in line. Don't worry. God has unexpected favor, unexpected promotion, unexpected turnarounds. You didn't see it coming, and it may seem as though your family will never come in or you could never set a new standard. You keep honoring God, and you will come into these moments when God has decided to bless you.

Far-and-Beyond Opportunities

I saw a young man on television who was playing professional football. He had just caught the game-winning touchdown. His teammates were piling on him, the fans were cheering, everybody was shouting and going wild. Two years earlier he had been working at a grocery store stocking shelves. He had been a star player in college and was excited about playing professionally, but he wasn't drafted. He had been turned down by all the teams. They said he was too small. No one wanted him. He felt overlooked, forgotten. He knew he had what it takes, but nobody would give him a chance. One day, out of the blue, a coach whom he had never met called and invited him to try out for the team. He made the team and went on to become their leading receiver. When the reporter was interviewing him after the game-winning catch, this young man thanked the Lord, then he said, "Wow! I never saw this coming." He thought his days of football were over. He'd already accepted that it wasn't meant to be, then God crossed His arms. Not only was he celebrating the victory, but everyone was celebrating him.

People may rule you out, they may tell you it's never going to work out, but God has the

> *People may rule you out, they may tell you it's never going to work out, but God has the final say.*

final say. He knows how to take you from the background to the foreground. When He decides to bless you, things are going to happen that you didn't see coming. You don't have to be the most qualified, the most experienced, or from the most influential family. If you are, that's great. God can still take you higher. You may feel that you have disadvantages, and some you have no control over—what family you were born into, what nationality, what social standing. Ephraim couldn't help it that he wasn't the firstborn son. He couldn't help it that his mother had worshipped idols. He had no say over that. On the surface, that could hold you back and cause you to think, *Too bad for me. This is my lot in life*, but God doesn't choose the way we choose. He's about to show you influence, ability, and opportunities that you didn't see coming.

David said, "Who am I, O Lord, and what is my family that You would take me this far?" He was saying, "I wasn't the biggest, strongest, or the most qualified. I didn't come from royalty. I was a shepherd working in the fields, minding my own business, and, Lord, look where You've taken me." He didn't have to go after it. It came after him. The prophet Samuel showed up at his house to anoint him king.

God has some far-and-beyond opportunities that are about to come looking for you. The right people are going to track you down. You couldn't make it happen. It's the arm of the Lord reaching down to promote, to elevate, to increase you. You're going to look back and say as David did, "Wow, God! I never dreamed You'd take me to this level." Now keep your faith out there. Thoughts will tell you it's never going to happen. Get ready. God's about to cross His arms. I believe and declare you're coming into unexpected favor, unexpected healing, unexpected turnarounds. God is going to take you from the background to the foreground. You're going to step into new levels and see His favor in greater ways.

CHAPTER TEN

Just One Good Break

Sometimes we don't see how we can accomplish our dreams. We don't have the connections, the resources, or the experience. I talked to a young man who wanted to go to college, but his scholarship didn't go through. He comes from a single-parent home and doesn't have the funds. The odds are against him, and it's easy to get discouraged in those situations and say, "I can't get out of debt. I've gone as far as I can." "I'll never get well. Look at the medical report." "I'll never break this addiction. I've had it for years."

It may look as though it's not going to happen, but what you can't see is you're just one good break away. Just meeting one right person, just one phone call, one contract, one healing, and what seemed impossible will suddenly become possible. You don't need a hundred things to go right. Just one touch of God's favor, and doors will open that you couldn't open. Just one person being for you will catapult you ahead. Just one breakthrough, and suddenly you get well. Suddenly you're free from the addiction. Suddenly the depression is gone. You may have situations that don't look as though they'll ever change, but stay encouraged. God has already arranged good breaks for you, things that you couldn't make happen. You weren't next in line. You didn't have the experience, but out of nowhere the contract came to you.

He's already lined up the right people to help you. You didn't ask them. You didn't have to try to win them over. For no apparent reason, they will go out of their way to be good to you. They've been ordained by God to move you into your destiny. You don't have to worry about how it's going to work out. God can cause one person to like you, one person to say, "Promote them. Give them the position," and suddenly you'll go to a new level. Instead of thinking, *It's a long way off. I don't see how it can ever happen*, turn it around and say, "Father, thank You that I'm just one good break away. Thank You that with one touch of Your goodness, things will change in my favor."

Just One Phone Call Away

Do you know how we got the Compaq Center? Just one phone call. That's how it all started. We were trying to build a new auditorium, but twice the properties we found were sold out from under us, and I was disappointed. We couldn't find any more land that was the size we needed. But when something doesn't work out your way, it's because God has something better in store. You may not be able to see it at that time, but that's when you have to trust Him. One afternoon I was at the office, minding my own business. A friend whom I hadn't spoken to in a couple years called and said, "Joel, I have an idea for you. Let's go to lunch." The next day at lunch he told me that the Rockets basketball team was moving out of the Compaq Center and that Lakewood should try to purchase it from the city. When I heard that, something came alive inside. I knew we were supposed to pursue it.

When I got back from lunch, I called the mayor. He was a friend of our family. I told him that we were interested. He said, "Joel, I think Lakewood having the Compaq Center would be great for the City of Houston." God knows how to have the right people be for you. When those two owners sold their properties out from under us, I didn't like it, it didn't seem fair; but the truth is, it wasn't their choice. It was the hand of God. They weren't supposed to be for us. If they would have done what I wanted, we would have missed out on the Compaq Center.

When somebody is not for you, don't get bent out of shape. God has the right people already lined up who will want to help you, people who are ordained to open doors that you couldn't open, people who will use their influence to thrust you ahead. But there were some people who didn't want us to have the Compaq Center, critics who said it wasn't a good fit, and they brought opposition and tried to stop us. However, the mayor was in charge of the city. He set the agenda. His being for us is what kept all the opposition from stopping us. Every time they tried to keep it from happening, he would adjust something in our favor and we kept moving forward. I've learned you don't need everyone to be for you. You just need the right people to be for you. It just so happened that the man who liked us was in charge. He ran the city. God is going to cause people to be for you who are in a position of authority, people who can override your critics, people who will cause things to fall into place.

> You don't need everyone to be for you. You just need the right people to be for you.

You may feel as if you're falling behind. You could never accomplish what God put in your heart. Don't worry. God knows how to make up for lost time. Other people discount you, don't give you credit. Don't worry. God knows how to make up for lost time. Just one touch of His favor will catapult you years ahead. Just one person opening a door, just one phone call out of the blue, and you look up and you're fifty years down the road. You're not in the metal building. You're in the Compaq Center. You're not in the run-down area. You're on the main freeway. People don't discount you anymore. Now they look up to you. God is going to cause you to be seen in a new light. He's going to give you respect, credibility, and influence that's going to make up for the time it looked as though you'd lost.

Those years when you were not being noticed, not seeing good breaks, not having much influence, those were proving years. You were showing God you could be trusted. You were doing the right thing when the wrong thing was happening, being your best when you weren't seeing growth, and going to work with a good attitude even though nobody was giving you credit. Those were important years. Without you being faithful and showing God that you could be trusted, you wouldn't be ready for what God has in store. You have to be prepared for where God is taking you. You're not falling behind. You're in training, and if it's taking longer than you thought, it's because God has something big in your future. Don't slack off. Don't get tired of doing the right thing. If you keep passing the test, the Scripture says, "Your due season is coming." That means God's not only going to bring you out, He's going to thrust you ahead. You're going to come out promoted, increased, and further than you've ever imagined.

Just One Person Away

As a teenager, David was out in the shepherds' fields taking care of his father's sheep. It was boring. David had big dreams in his heart. He knew he was going to leave his mark, but year after year all he did was feed the sheep, clean up their waste, and make sure they were protected and healthy. It was a dirty, smelly, lonely job. Nobody thanked him. Nobody knew that he'd killed a lion and a bear to protect those animals. He could've slacked off, had a bad attitude, and said, "God, it's not fair. I'm wasting time out here."

Instead, he kept passing the test, doing the right thing when nothing was changing. One day the prophet Samuel came to his house to anoint the next king of Israel. He looked at David's seven older brothers, who had more experience and training. Some of them were in the military. They were bigger, stronger, and more muscular than David. They looked like kings. Samuel passed by them and eventually came to David, the forgotten one, the one who had been overlooked, discounted, seen as less than. Samuel said, "This is the next king of Israel." I'm sure his brothers and his parents nearly passed out. "You mean David, the shepherd, the youngest, the smallest? Are you sure?"

God doesn't choose the way people choose. People look on the outside. God looks on the heart. God found a man in David whom He could trust, a man who had proven he'd be faithful when things weren't going his way. God knew that if He could trust him to take care of sheep, He could trust him to take care of His people. When God promoted David and brought him out of the shepherds' fields, He made up for all the years it looked as though David was losing out. David went from being a shepherd to being the next king. Nobody voted for him. This wasn't a democracy. If it had been, he wouldn't have received one vote.

> *David went from being a shepherd to being the next king.*

He wasn't on anyone's radar. Nobody in Israel knew who he was. His father didn't believe in him. His brothers tried to belittle him.

When God is ready to promote you, He doesn't take a vote. He doesn't check to see who likes you, who's for you, how popular you are. It's not a vote. It's an appointment. It's up to one person—not your boss, not your neighbors, not your critics, not your relatives. Promotion doesn't come from people. It comes from the Lord. When it's your time to be promoted, no person, no bad break, no disappointment, and no enemy can stop you. God has the one and only vote. He has the final say.

Now quit worrying about who's not for you. "Why won't these people give me credit? Joel, I'd be further along if my coworkers would quit leaving me out." Can I tell you that your coworkers can't hold you back? Other people cannot keep you from your destiny. They didn't know you before you were formed in your mother's womb. They didn't lay out the plan for your life. They didn't crown you with favor. They didn't put seeds of greatness inside you. Quit focusing on who's not for you, and start focusing on Who is for you. The Most High God, the Creator of the universe, the One who spoke worlds into existence is breathing in your direction. He has you in the palms of His hands. His plans for you are for good. His being for you is more than the world being against you.

David's life was set on a new course by just one person. When Samuel came to his house and anointed him king, his whole world changed. What's interesting is that David didn't have to go after Samuel. Samuel came after David. You don't have to go after the blessing. Keep honoring God, and the blessing will come to you. The phone call will come to you. The Compaq Center will come to you. The right person, the healing, the promotion will find you. We spend too much time trying to make things happen. Then we get frustrated because it's taking so long. But you can't make things happen that are out of God's timing. You can't make people like you who are not supposed to like you. You can't open a door that God has closed.

Don't Want What's Not Supposed to Be Yours

I tried twice to buy the property to build a new sanctuary. I did my best. I was nice to those two owners. I smiled my biggest smile. I thanked them in advance for selling it to us. No matter how charming I was or how much money we offered, that door wasn't going to open. Stay in peace, knowing that God will cause the right people to find you. The right breaks will track you down. The right opportunities will come knocking at your door. When it's your time, Samuel will show up. David's father tried to convince Samuel to anoint one of his other seven sons. He thought David was too small, too young, too inexperi-

> *The right breaks will track you down. The right opportunities will come knocking at your door.*

enced. But no matter how hard he tried, Samuel wouldn't do it. God was showing us that what has your name on it won't go to anyone else. Quit being upset because that coworker got the promotion you really wanted. If it was supposed to be yours, you would have it. Or that friend who married the man you really liked—that didn't seem fair. But if you were supposed to marry him, then she wouldn't have. That you didn't means that God has somebody better for you.

I've learned that you don't want what's not supposed to be yours. There's no grace for it. One time I wanted a business opportunity so badly. I did everything I could to make it happen. Sometimes God will close a door that we can't open, but there are times when, if we're really stubborn and it's not going to stop our destiny, God will let us have it our way. In this case, we obtained the business, but it wasn't what I thought. It was a constant headache, it never really got off the ground, and it drained our time, energy, and resources. Now my attitude is, *God, if it doesn't have my name on it, I don't want it.* If it's not supposed to be yours, you're not going to have a grace for it. Don't try to beat the door down. Be determined, pursue your dreams, but be smart enough to realize that what God wants to be yours will come to you. It won't be a constant struggle. Yes, there'll be opposition. Yes, you'll have to work hard. You'll have to fight the good fight of faith, but there will be a grace that causes things to fall into place.

The psalmist said, "God will work out His plan for your life." You don't have to work it out. You don't have to struggle, live worried, try to fix every problem, straighten out every enemy, make everything happen in your own strength.

You can live from a place of rest, knowing that God is not only fighting your battles, but He's lined up the breaks you need. He has the right people who will help you. He has solutions to problems that you can't see right now. He's already figured out how to solve it. Don't waste your time worrying. He's on the throne. He can see things you can't see. He's promised He will work out His plan for your life.

Just One Change of Mind Away

I received a letter from a young woman who lives in Africa. Her dream was to get her doctorate degree so she could become a college professor. She'd finished her master's degree and was preparing for the final exams to get into the doctorate program when her landlord broke her lease and told her she had to move out of the apartment where she was living. In just a couple days, she had to leave that place and move into the dorm. This all happened in the middle of final exams. It threw her off, and she couldn't study as she had hoped. She ended up being turned down by the university that she wanted to attend. She was not only disappointed in herself, but she was angry at the landlord for making her leave, especially at that time. She was about to meet with an attorney and take legal action against him, but she always listens to our podcast. My message that week was called "You Have a Defender," in which I talked about how we all have unfair things happen, but God wouldn't allow it if He wasn't going to somehow use it for our good. I also talked about how God can vindicate us better than we can vindicate ourselves. She knew that was God speaking to her, and she let the anger and the lawsuit go.

After being turned down by sixteen universities, she applied to a very prestigious university in Italy. They really liked her, but they had twelve people on the waiting list ahead of her, and they told her that unfortunately she wouldn't be accepted. Two weeks later, they emailed back and said, "We've never done this before, but we've changed our mind and opened up a position just for you." When she arrived, they informed her that out of hundreds of doctorate students, she was one of the six chosen to be in the advanced studies program. That meant she would not only receive a full scholarship, but she wouldn't have to live in the dorm. She would have her own executive apartment in a beautiful neighborhood close to the university. Her thoughts went back to the man who'd broken the lease, making her leave her apartment, and how she'd thought that was setting her back when, in fact, it was setting her up. God knows how to work out His plan for your life. It may not seem as though it's going to happen, but you're just one good break away from a university saying, "We've changed our mind," just one good break away from Samuel showing up, just one good break away from a phone call saying, "Hey, the Compaq Center's available." You'll look back and say as she did, "Wow, God! You've amazed me with Your goodness."

David said, "I have pitched my tent in the land of hope."

My question is, Where have you pitched your tent? "Well, Joel, I've had a lot of disappointments." "I'll never get well." "I can't accomplish my dreams. It's been too long." The problem is not that God can't do it. The problem is where you've pitched your tent. As long as you're thinking of all the reasons why it's not going to happen, how impossible it is, that's going to limit you. Why don't you do yourself a favor, pull up your stakes, pick up your tent, and move out of the land of doubt, negativity, and self-pity? Move out of the land of "It can't happen. I'm too old. I never get any good breaks." That's the wrong neighborhood. Get out of that place and pitch your tent in the land of "With God all things are possible," the land of "Goodness and mercy are chasing me down," the land of "What was meant for my harm God is turning to my advantage." You are just one good break away from God catapulting you to a new level. Just one right person showing you favor will change the course of your life. Just one touch of God's goodness and you'll beat the cancer. You'll break the addiction. You'll see your family restored.

You are just one good break away from God catapulting you to a new level.

Just One Day Away

In Acts 3, there was a man who had been crippled since birth. Every day his family would carry him to the temple and set him beside the gate so he could beg. He'd been doing this for years. One day Peter and John came walking by. The man held out his cup, wanting some coins. Peter said, "I'm sorry, we don't have any money for you, but in the name of Jesus, rise and walk." Peter took him by the hand and pulled the man up. Instantly he was healed. He was so excited that he took off running through the temple, thanking God.

Here's my point. When the man woke up that morning, he thought it was just another ordinary day. He'd go to the temple, sit by the gate, and beg, just as he'd done for years. He'd had no idea when he went to bed the night before that he soon would be able to walk. He didn't realize he was just one good break away from having his whole life changed. Just one person ordained by God to speak healing, and he would do something he was told he could never do.

You may have some big obstacles in your path today, things that have held you back for a long time—a sickness, an addiction, depression, loneliness. It doesn't seem as though it'll ever change. You could get comfortable and accept it. No, get ready. God is about to surprise you. He's already spoken to the right people. He's already lined up the healing, the freedom, the promotion. It's going to happen suddenly. You didn't see it coming. You woke up one morning expecting more of the same. You never dreamed when you went to bed that night before that you would be healed, free, promoted, vindicated. The good news is, it could happen today. It could happen this week. This month, your whole world could change for the better. Now do your part. Pitch your tent in the land of hope. Give God something to work with. That's not just being positive. That's your faith being released.

When the people in the temple saw this man running and celebrating, they looked at one another and said, "Isn't that the guy who's been begging by the gate for the last forty years?" They couldn't believe it. The Scripture says, "They were astonished." God has some things in your future that are not only going to leave you amazed, but people around you are going to be amazed. You were not created to live in dysfunction, with addictions, and to be constantly struggling. That may be how it's been in the past, but that's not how it's going to be in the future. God's about to do a new thing. He's going to break bondages that have held you back. He's going to free you from those addictions. He's going to increase you to where you have more than enough. That sickness is not permanent. Healing is coming. Wholeness is on the way. Victory is in your future.

Just One Touch Away

I talked to a young man who was on dialysis. He was in his early thirties. He had to spend three days a week, four hours a day, in the clinic. My father was on dialysis at the end of his life, and I took him to the clinic a lot. You don't see many people on dialysis who are in their thirties. My heart went out to him because that's not an easy thing. He told me how he had had this problem since childhood, and he wasn't a candidate for a kidney transplant. He had a great attitude and went to work every day. We prayed that God would not only help him fulfill his destiny, but that God would make a way where we didn't see a way. When I saw him a couple years later, he said, "Joel, you'll never believe what happened." For years the doctors had told him that he couldn't have a transplant, but one doctor took a special interest in him, studied his case, and said, "I can see why nobody wants to take the risk, but this is what I specialize in." One night, at one o'clock in the morning, he received a phone call from the doctor, saying, "Be at the hospital tomorrow morning at six. I have a kidney for you." The man was beaming with joy. He said, "Joel, I'm not on dialysis anymore. I have a new kidney."

One touch of God's favor, one doctor going out of his way to be good to him, and that young man's whole world changed. What you're facing may look as though it's never going to change. People have told you, "No, the odds are against you." Can I tell you, you're just one good break away? Just one touch of God's favor, and suddenly you'll get well. Suddenly you'll get the kidney. Suddenly you'll be free. Suddenly you'll be promoted. I'm asking you to pitch your tent in the land of hope. Get up every morning with expectancy, knowing that the Most High God is working out His plan for your life. If you do this, I believe and declare that God is about to surprise you. He's going to make things happen that you didn't see coming. Suddenly healing, breakthroughs, and the right people.

CHAPTER ELEVEN

By This Time Next Year

We all face challenges that look permanent, as if they'll never turn around, dreams and goals that seem as though they're a long way off. It's easy to get discouraged and accept that it's never going to work out. But what you can't see is God is working behind the scenes. What He promised you, He still has every intention of bringing to pass.

All the circumstances may say it's going to take years to get out of debt, years to meet the right person, but God is going to surprise you. It's going to happen sooner than it looks. There wasn't any sign of it. You weren't expecting it. Out of nowhere, your health improves, your business takes off, you break the addiction. Don't believe the lies that it's permanent. You may not see anything changing yet, but stay in faith; you are closer than you think.

It May Seem Too Good to Be True

In 2 Kings 4, there was a wealthy lady who lived in the town of Shunem. When the prophet Elisha came through, she would invite him to come to dinner with her and her husband. She could sense there was something special about Elisha. She told her husband, "He's a man of God. We need to take care of him." So she had a room built on top of her house, a guest suite so Elisha could stay there when he was in town. She could have just kept inviting him to dinner, which would have been nice. She could have rented him a room at the local inn, which would have been kind. But this lady went to great lengths to take care of Elisha. He had his own room on the roof of her house, with a beautiful bed, windows, and nice carpet.

One day Elisha was in town, resting in that bed. He began to think about how kind the lady was and how she'd gone to great expense to make sure he was comfortable. He said to his assistant, "Go ask her what she wants me to do for her. Ask if she wants me to put in a good word for her to the commander of the army." When he asked her, she said, "I don't need anything. We live in peace and security and don't need any special favors. We're blessed. We're healthy. Life is good." You might think Elisha would say, "All right, I tried my best. I'm glad this lady is blessed." But Elisha was determined to do something for her and didn't stop there.

He asked his assistant, "What do you think I can do for her?" He said, "The only thing I can think of is that she's never had children. She's been barren her whole life, and her husband is old." Elisha said, "Call her. I want to speak to her." The lady came to the doorway, and Elisha said, "By this time next year, you're going to be holding a son in your arms." She nearly passed out. That was her dream. She said, "Sir, please, don't lie to me like that." Even though she thought it was too good to be true, even though she didn't really believe, a year later she gave birth to a healthy son. I could imagine that the bed she built for the prophet now held her little baby boy. She never dreamed that room she'd added to take care of the man of God would one day be used for her own child.

When you give to take care of God's work, when you're generous with your tithes and offerings as this lady was, God will always take care of you. You cannot give God something without Him giving you more back in return. This lady didn't need anything. She was blessed and happy, but God won't allow you to just be a giver. When you give, it will come back to you good measure, pressed down, and running over. This lady had already accepted that she couldn't have children. It was too late. She had missed her window of opportunity, but God is not limited by the natural. He's a supernatural God. He can make things happen out of season.

What You Can't Buy

It may look as though you could never have a baby, never accomplish a dream, never get out of debt. God is saying to you what He said to the lady from Shunem, "By this time next year, you're going to see things happen that you never dreamed would happen." The medical report may not look good, but God can do what medicine cannot do. By this time next year, you could be cancer free. You've been single a long time; get ready. By this time next year, you could be happily married. Business is slow; stay encouraged. By this time next year, you could be out of debt.

"Not me, Joel. You should see my finances." You should see my God. One touch of His favor will put you into overflow. When you read this, it can sound too good to be true. That's the way this lady felt. She said, in effect, "Elisha, don't get my hopes up. You know how long I've dreamed of having a baby." Her mind told her that it wasn't going to happen, but down in her spirit, something whispered, "This is for you. Receive it. Your baby is on the way." Your mind will tell you all the reasons why you won't get well or how you can't get out of debt, especially in a year. You think it's going to take thirty years. Your mind may say no, but if you'll

Your mind may say no, but if you'll listen down in your spirit, you will hear that still, small voice saying, "Yes, it is on the way."

listen down in your spirit, you will hear that still, small voice saying, "Yes, it is on the way."

I talked to a lady who had a child born prematurely. Her son spent the first year of his life in the hospital. She has insurance, but it didn't cover the full amount. The part she owed was three million dollars, and while she was so grateful that her son was alive, she's a schoolteacher. It looked as though she would be paying on that debt for her whole life. Just recently she received a letter from the board of directors of the hospital that read: "We have decided to forgive your three-million-dollar debt." If that lady had read this chapter before she received the letter, she would have thought, *Joel, you have the wrong person. Me, out of debt in a year? That's not possible.* But if you asked her today, she would tell you that God can do the impossible. Just because you don't see a way doesn't mean God doesn't have a way. It's because He's going to do it out of the ordinary; it will be unusual, you won't see it coming.

Our part is to do as the Shunammite lady did in the Scripture and be a giver, have a generous spirit. When you're always being a blessing, God will make sure that you're always blessed. I don't mean just with material things. God can give you what money cannot buy. This lady already had wealth and influence, she knew the right people, but she didn't have children. God said to her, in effect, "I'm going to give you something you can't buy. Here's a son." God can bring you a divine connection, somebody in your life to love. You can't buy that. God can give you peace in your mind so you can lie down at night and sleep well. You can't purchase that. Perhaps you're fighting an illness. Every report says it's permanent, and you've been told to just learn to live with it. Receive this into your spirit: By this time next year, you're going to be healthy, whole, back on your feet, enjoying life. "Well, Joel, how could that be possible? The medical report says there's no way." There's another report: God says He is restoring health back to you. He says the number of your days, He will fulfill.

It's Going to Happen

I heard a story about a twelve-year-old girl who had a rare form of incurable cancer. Instead of going to school and playing with her friends, she spent her days in the hospital, very sick. It didn't look as though she would make it much longer. But some researchers received approval to use an experimental drug that they had never tried on people. She took the treatment, and after two months, the cancer started to shrink. Six months later, she was able to go back to school. At the age of fourteen, against all odds, she was cancer free. But if you had told this young lady while she was in the hospital with terminal cancer, "By this time next year, you're going to be back at school, with no cancer, full of energy, and enjoying life," she could have thought, *That's not possible. It's never happened with this type of cancer.* But God has the final say. You may think your marriage is beyond restoring, you've had the addiction so long you could never break it, you'll never get well, you'll never meet the right person, but God is saying, "By this time next year, it's going to happen."

For dreams that look as though they'll take a lifetime to accomplish, get ready. It's going to happen sooner than you think. Things are about to fall into place. The right people are going to find you. Good breaks are going to track you down. You wouldn't be reading this if God wasn't about to do something amazing, something out of the ordinary. When we were trying to find property to build a new sanctuary, the doors kept closing. Everything fell through, and I didn't see any more options. I didn't think we could keep growing. We looked as if we were stuck. We didn't have any more room. Back then when I was so discouraged, if you had told me that by this time next year, we would have a building already built on the main freeway, one of the most recognized buildings in the city, the Compaq Center, I would have thought, *There's no way. How could that happen?* That was so far out of my thinking. But even though I couldn't fathom it didn't mean it didn't happen. Look where we are today.

Some of these things you may not be able to see yet. It seems too far out, so unlikely, but our God is so great that it doesn't mean it's going to keep Him from doing it. Because you honor Him, as this lady in the Scripture did, God is not only going to do more than you can imagine, but it's going to happen sooner than you think. It is not going to take your whole lifetime to accomplish the dream

> *By this time next year, you're going to be amazed at where you are.*

God put in your heart. By this time next year, you're going to be amazed at where you are. If you had told me when I was twenty-two years old and single, playing baseball every night and never really having dated anyone, that by that time next year, I would be engaged to a beautiful, talented, fun, hot, fine, good-looking girl named Victoria, I wouldn't have believed it. But that didn't stop God from doing it. Thirty-two years later, we're still married, and I'm still just as good-looking—I mean, she's still just as good-looking.

God has some of these "by this time next year" moments lined up for you where you're going to look back and say, "Wow! I never dreamed I'd have this position, never dreamed my children would be doing this great, never dreamed I could build that orphanage." Get ready for God to show out in your life.

You Can't Dream This Up

When I was growing up, our family knew this very successful businessman. He'd built his company into a global brand that was known all over the world. His name was the company's name. He was very well respected and influential, but later in his career the economy went down and his business slowed. After years of being successful and seeing blessings, it looked as though he would end his career having to close his business with his reputation tarnished. He was in his late eighties and was millions of dollars in debt. It didn't look as though there was any way he could pay it. At his lowest moment when it looked so impossible, when he didn't think it could ever work out, he received a phone call out of the blue. A man from another company said, "We'd like to purchase your company. We'll pay off all the debt. We'll renovate all the facilities, and we'll keep your name to honor your legacy." That company spent over a hundred million dollars renovating their headquarters. Today that business is thriving more than ever. But if you had told this man in the middle of the downturn when it seemed so impossible that "By this time next year, you will not only be out of debt but your business will be flourishing and your legacy will continue on," he couldn't have fathomed it. He never dreamed it would turn out that good.

As with this man, some of these things that seem so impossible, that seem so far out to you, by this time next year, you're going to be amazed. You couldn't make it happen. It is the hand of God on your life.

Think about Joseph, sitting in a prison for twelve years after having been betrayed by his brothers, then falsely accused by the boss's wife—one bad break after another. There was nothing in his circumstances that looked as if he would ever accomplish his dream of ruling a nation. It looked just the opposite. If Joseph had heard me on the television or radio, he could have said, "Joel, I appreciate your encouragement, but I'm in prison. I'm a slave. I had no trial. I have no lawyer. I don't have anyone to stand up for me."

Your time is coming.

He could have been discouraged. I believe that deep down Joseph could hear this still, small voice saying, "This is not your destiny. Your time is coming."

One day the guard came over and told Joseph that Pharaoh wanted to see him. Joseph went in and interpreted Pharaoh's dream. Pharaoh was so impressed that he made Joseph the prime minister of Egypt. God has already lined up people in positions of influence who will open doors you couldn't open, bring you opportunities and promotion that you didn't see coming. As was true for Joseph, you don't have to find them, they will find you. But if you told Joseph while he was sitting in prison after twelve years of bad breaks and injustice that by this time next year, he was going to be second in command of the nation instead of being in prison, that he was going to be in charge, respected, admired, and have people serving him, he could have thought, *Are you kidding? Do you see these bars I'm behind? Do you realize the boss's wife is against me?* It's one thing to have a man against you, but when you have a woman mad at you and she happens to be married to your boss, you are going to need a miracle.

You may be in one of these unfair situations that seem as though it's never going to turn around. God is saying, "By this time next year, it's going to change. By this time next year, you're going to be vindicated, promoted, in a position of honor." Why are you worrying? Why are you losing sleep? God is still on the throne. He hasn't forgotten about you. Your time is coming. This looks like a stumbling block that you can't get past. The truth is, it's a stepping-stone that's about to take you to a new level of your destiny.

Get Your Hopes Up

In the Scripture, a man named Haman worked for the king of Persia. He had a very influential position, but he let it go to his head. All the people would bow down before him except for a Jewish man named Mordecai, who was a relative of Queen Esther. He knew it was only right to bow down before God. This made Haman so upset that he went to the king and said, "There's a group of people who don't obey your commands. They're troublemakers, and they need to be killed." He convinced the king to issue a decree that on a certain date all the Jews throughout the kingdom should be killed.

But one night the king couldn't sleep. He asked his assistant to bring him the book of the chronicles that recorded the history of his reign. The assistant brought the book and started reading accounts to the king at random. There just so happened to be a recording of how Mordecai had exposed a conspiracy to assassinate the king. The king was so impressed that the next morning he called Haman in and said, "Haman, what do you think we should do for a man whom I delight to honor and has never been recognized by the city?" Haman was so arrogant that he thought the king was talking about him, so he played it up really big. He said, "King, I think we should put a royal robe on him, have a big parade and someone should march him on a horse up and down the streets while proclaiming what a great man he is." The king said, "I love that idea. Now go find Mordecai the Jew, and you do for him just what you said." It was an amazing setback and humiliation to Haman.

Meanwhile, Queen Esther set up a meeting with the king and Haman and she exposed what Haman was really trying to do. Instead of getting rid of all the Jews, the king got rid of Haman. He sent out another decree that overruled the first decree, and he gave Mordecai the position Haman had occupied. If you had told Mordecai in the middle of the trouble, when it looked as though the Jews would be annihilated, that by this time next year Haman was going to be gone, the king's original decree was going to be overruled, and he was going to be in a position of honor, he could have thought, *That's too good to be true. How could all that possibly happen?* God has ways that we've never thought of.

You may be in a difficult situation, people are coming against you, your finances don't look good, there's trouble in a relationship. You could be upset and worried, but stay in peace. It is not permanent. As with Mordecai, by this time next year, it's all going to be turned in your favor. Because you honor God, He's dealing with those enemies. He's fighting your battles. Those people who are trying to stop you are not going to succeed. It looks as if they have the upper hand, they have more authority, and they may be over you, but the good news is that our God is over them. He controls the universe. Keep doing the right thing. Don't take matters into your own hands. Let God be your vindicator, and by this time next year the enemies you see today you will see no more. By this time next year, what was meant for your harm will be turned to your advantage.

"Now, Joel, this is encouraging, but I don't see how it can happen for me." Neither did Mordecai, neither did Joseph, and neither did that twelve-year-old girl. You don't have to see how it can happen; all you have to do is believe. When you believe, angels go to work.

> *You don't have to see how it can happen; all you have to do is believe.*

When you believe, forces of darkness are pushed back. When you believe, things begin to change in your favor.

I talked to a man who had been in prison since he was seventeen years old. He was convicted of selling drugs and sentenced to forty years. He'd been watching our television broadcast in prison with the other inmates, and he'd given his life to Christ. He had a whole new outlook on his life. In one message he heard me talk about how God is going to do things sooner than expected. That took root down in his spirit. He started telling the other inmates that he was going to get out soon. They looked at him as if he wasn't all there. He had twenty-five more years left. Six months later, the warden called him in and said, "Because of good behavior, we're going to commute the rest of your sentence. You are free to go." The other prisoners looked at him as if to say, "Will you pray for us?" He was released recently, and the first place he came to was Lakewood. He flew here from another city. When I met him, he had big tears running down his cheeks. He was so grateful, so overcome with emotion, he could hardly speak.

As with him, by this time next year, you're going to see things happen that you never dreamed would happen. By this time next year, you're going to be at a new level in your health, in your finances, in your career. By this time next year, you're going to be free from that addiction. God is up to something. He's about to show out in your life. "Well, Joel, you're just getting people's hopes up. I don't think this is going to happen for me." You're right; it's not going to happen. This is for people who believe. You have to let the seed take root. Here's the key: Don't talk yourself out of it. Talk yourself into it.

Sooner Than You Think

In 2 Kings 7, the Syrian army had surrounded the city of Samaria and cut off the Israelites' food supply. The people were starving and beyond desperate. It looked as though it was the end. The prophet Elisha showed up and said to the Israelites, "By this time tomorrow, there will be so much food that you can buy bread for a penny a loaf." People looked at Elisha as though he had lost his mind. They were surrounded, starving to death—it seemed impossible. One of the main leaders said, "Elisha, even if God opened the windows of Heaven, that still wouldn't happen."

There were four lepers sitting outside the city gates of Samaria. They said to one another, "We have nothing to lose. We're going to die anyway. Let's walk over to the enemy's camp and surrender. If they spare us, we live." They started walking toward the camp, and God multiplied the sound of their footsteps. The Syrians thought a huge army was coming to attack them. They panicked and took off running for their lives, leaving behind all their food, their supplies, and even their gold and silver. The lepers went back and told the Israelites, "It's just as Elisha said. There is so much food that you could buy a loaf of bread for one penny."

"Joel, I thought you said by this time next year." Yes, but God also has some of these "by this time tomorrow" moments. It may not take a full year. God knows how to accelerate things. It's going to happen sooner than you think. You are closer than it looks. All the circumstances may say, "It's impossible. You could never get well that soon. Your business could never turn around overnight. You can't break the addiction by tomorrow. It's going to take years." You don't know what God is up to. You're looking at it in the natural. We serve a supernatural God. Don't be like that one leader in Samaria and think of all the reasons why it can't happen. Get in agreement with God. Believe something good is on the way. All through the day, thank Him that He's working in your life. If you do this, I believe and declare as Elisha did to the barren lady, "By this time next year, you're going to have your baby. That dream is going to come to pass. That problem is going to be resolved."

CHAPTER TWELVE

Commanded to Be Blessed

When we honor God with our lives and do our best to keep Him first place, the Scripture says God will command His blessing to come on us. When God commands, it's not "maybe it will happen," or "I hope it happens," or "if the circumstances come together." No, when God commands, there are no ifs, ands, or buts about it. It's going to happen.

When God said, "Let there be light," the Earth was dark, without form, like a black hole. But God didn't check the circumstances to see if light was possible. He didn't have experts analyze it to see if they thought it could happen. He simply spoke the words. When He commanded the light, it came at 186,000 miles per second, and nothing could stop it. In a similar way, when God commands you to be blessed, He doesn't check what family you come from, where you work, who likes you, or how good the economy is. None of that matters to God. All the circumstances can be against you. The experts may tell you, "You'll never get well. You'll never meet the right person. You'll never be successful." Every voice says, "You're stuck. Just accept it. There's no way in the natural." The good news is, we serve a supernatural God. When He commands the blessing, all the forces of darkness cannot stop Him.

With the commanded blessing, you'll go places you couldn't go on your own. Doors will open that you couldn't open. You'll be promoted even though you weren't the most qualified. The commanded blessing will cause good breaks to find you. Contracts, opportunities, business, and favor will track you down. Now get in agreement with God. Quit saying, "I'll never get ahead, Joel. These people at work don't like me." It doesn't matter who doesn't like you at work. What matters is that the Most High God likes you, and He is not limited by who's against you, by who's not giving you credit, by who's not treating you right. One touch of His favor will move them out of the way and get you to where you're supposed to be. Don't be discouraged by what's unfair. God sees what's happening. Keep being your best; keep honoring Him. You're not working unto people, you're working unto God, and when it's your time to be promoted, rest assured you will be promoted. People can't stop you. Bad breaks can't stop you. Injustice can't stop you. The commanded blessing on your life will override every force that's trying to hold you back.

I know a young man who works in the medical field. He graduated from college and had been at the same entry-level position in his company for six years. He's a hard worker and always does more than required, but his supervisor never liked him. He wouldn't give him any credit and kept promoting new employees over him who didn't have his training or expertise. It wasn't fair, and he didn't like it, but he understands this principle: Because he's honoring God, there is a commanded blessing on his life. One morning he went to work and found out that his supervisor had unexpectedly resigned. He had a family issue and had to move to another state. The administration called him in and said, "This supervisor has recommended you to take his position." The supervisor never even liked him and was never for him, but when you have the commanded blessing, God will cause people to be good to you who have never been good to you. He'll use even your enemies to bless you. This young man was so excited and so baffled at the same time. He said, "Joel, this man tried to hold me down. He tried to discredit me."

Here's the key: People don't have the final say; God does. People don't determine your destiny. They didn't breathe life into you, they didn't call you, and they didn't number your days. You may be in a situation that feels unfair, where it seems as though somebody is stopping you. Don't worry. Your time is coming. Keep doing the right thing when the wrong thing is happening. There is a commanded blessing on your life. They can't keep you down. All the circumstances may be against you, but the Most High God is for you.

> *Don't worry. Your time is coming. Keep doing the right thing when the wrong thing is happening.*

Speak the Blessing

In Numbers 22, the Israelites were camped on the plains of Moab, headed toward Jericho. When the king of the Moabites saw how many Israelites there were, he was afraid. There was a prophet named Balaam who lived in a nearby city. The king knew that the Lord always did what Balaam asked, so he sent some of his men with a large amount of money to offer Balaam as a payment for him to come and curse the people of Israel. Balaam said, "I'll pray about it, but I can only say what God tells me to say." When he prayed, God said, "You are not to go with them, for what I have blessed you cannot curse."

Notice that when God puts the commanded blessing on you, it doesn't matter what somebody says, doesn't matter what they do or how they treat you. All that matters is that God put His blessing on you and everything else is of no effect. They can say it, but if you don't allow it to take root, it's not going to stop you. It may be unfair, it may seem as though it's getting the best of you, but if you stay in faith, the blessing will always override the curse. They meant it to stop you; God will use it to promote you.

The king's representatives went back and told the king that Balaam wouldn't come. The king said, "Send more distinguished officials, take more money, go back, and tell him he has to come and curse the Israelites." They went back, but Balaam said, "Even if the king gave me all the silver and gold in his palace, I am powerless to do anything against the will of my God." They spent the night there, and during the night the Lord told Balaam to go with them, but to do only what He told him. When he arrived, the king said, "Balaam, what took you so long? You should have come immediately. I need you to curse these people." Balaam said, "I'll pray again, but I can only say what the Lord tells me to say." After making an elaborate sacrifice, Balaam met with the Lord, who gave him this word for the king: "This is what the Lord says. The Israelites will succeed and become a great nation. They will have descendants too numerous to count." The king said, "Balaam, stop! What have you done to me? I brought you here to curse them, but instead you're blessing them." Balaam said it again, "I cannot curse what God has already blessed."

If Balaam were here today, he would say the same thing to you: "You cannot be cursed. There is a commanded blessing on your life." When you go through disappointments, unfair things happen; it's easy to feel that's clouded your future. Have a new perspective. What God has blessed, nothing can curse. When you understand you have this commanded blessing, you won't be upset because someone's talking about you. You won't be worried about your finances or discouraged because of a setback. You know every force that's trying to stop you is powerless to change the blessing God put on your life.

I love how when Balaam was supposed to curse the Israelites, and they were going to pay him a lot of money, not only did he refuse to do it, but God had him start speaking blessings over His people. He started telling how the Israelites were going to succeed, and go further, and accomplish great things. This is a spiritual principle that God was showing us. When the enemy tells you all the reasons why you're not going to get well, not get out of debt, not overcome the challenge, instead of agreeing with him, do as Balaam did and start speaking victory—speak health, speak favor, speak abundance.

The enemy wants you to curse your future with negative words and negative thoughts. He knows he can't stop you, but if he can convince you to go around discouraged, thinking you've reached your limits, that will keep you from your destiny. You have to turn it around. Tell the enemy, "You want me to curse my future? I know better. I'm going to bless my future." "Well, you'll never get out of debt, and you'll always struggle." "No, thanks. You have the wrong person. I will lend and not borrow. Whatever I touch will prosper and succeed. I've been commanded to be blessed." When he whispers, "You saw the medical report. You're never going to get well. Come on, agree with me. Curse your future." Turn it around and declare, "God is restoring health back to me. The number of my days, He will fulfill." "Well, the more you pray, the worse your child gets." "No, thanks. As for me and my house, we will serve the Lord. The seed of the righteous, my seed, will be mighty in the land." You

> *Tell the enemy, "You want me to curse my future? I know better. I'm going to bless my future."*

may have a lot coming against you; every voice says, "It's not going to work out." I'm asking you to be a Balaam and speak the blessing and not the curse.

Nothing Can Stop You

Sometimes it's not our own thoughts trying to discourage us, it's what other people are saying. People will tell you what you're not going to be, how you're not going to get well, how your dreams aren't going to come to pass. Here's the key: They can speak defeat all day long, but they are powerless to change the blessing on your life. Nothing they say or do can remove the blessing. They didn't give you the blessing, and they can't take it away. It was put on you by the God who spoke worlds into existence, and He didn't just give you the blessing, He commanded the blessing. There's a freedom when you understand this. When somebody's speaking badly about you, your attitude should be, *It's no big deal. They are powerless to stop the blessing on my life.* "Well, you had a bad break. You were laid off." "Yes, but I'm not worried. I know the blessing always overrides the curse." "Well, you come from a rough neighborhood. It doesn't look as though you have much of a future." "No, where I am is not where I'm staying. The commanded blessing will get me to where I'm supposed to be."

I talked with a woman who was raised in a dysfunctional environment. She was abused by her father. He constantly told her that she was no good and worthless, that she would never amount to anything. She was just a little girl; she didn't know any better. She believed the lies and grew up feeling ashamed and inferior. At seven years old, she was taken away from her father by the state and placed in foster home after foster home, never feeling loved or accepted. She grew up to become a young lady hooked on drugs, in bad relationships, having several children from different fathers, and living in poverty. It didn't look as though it would ever change. But in her late twenties, a friend invited her to church and she gave her life to Christ. She started making better decisions, doing her best to honor God. She would listen to our messages about reprogramming your mind and not believing the lies that people have spoken over you. It didn't happen overnight, but little by little things started to change in her favor. She was able to go back and finish high school in her early thirties. A friend helped her get into college, where a professor went out of her way to help open the door to nursing school. A hospital administrator showed her favor and hired her over several other candidates who had more qualifications. Today she's in charge of her whole department, supervising several hundred nurses at a large hospital. What happened? She came into the commanded blessing.

> The commanded blessing will override every person who's tried to stop you.

The commanded blessing will override every person who's tried to stop you. The commanded blessing will make up for what you didn't get. It will cause people to go out of their way to be good to you. It will put you at the right place at the right time. People may have tried to push you down, but God is about to lift you up. They may try to keep you from your purpose, but they are powerless to change the blessing on your life. You may have a lot coming against you, but I believe God is about to command some things. As He did for her, He's going to command justice, vindication, and deliverance from people who are not treating you right. He's going to command increase, promotion, and doors to open that take you to the next level. He's going to command freedom, breakthroughs, and wholeness. That addiction and those bad habits are not your destiny. He's about to command healing, restoration, and strength. That sickness is coming to an end. It may not have happened yet, but this is a new day. You're going to see the commanded blessing show out in your life. God is going to make things happen that amaze you, things you didn't see coming.

The Blessings Will Come to You

The Scripture says, "When you obey, God's blessings will chase you down and overtake you." I've seen this in my own life. Most of the big breaks, the major events, came to me. I didn't go after them. I was just honoring God, being my best, and they came after me. I didn't know the Compaq Center was coming available, but a man came to me out of the blue and said, "Joel, you need to call the mayor. That should be Lakewood's building." A publisher whom I had never met came to me and said, "I want to publish your books." SiriusXM Radio came to me and said, "Here's a satellite radio channel." That's the commanded blessing. God will cause opportunities, favor, and contracts to chase you down.

Here's the key: You don't have to go after the blessing; go after God. Honor Him with your life, and the blessing will follow. God will command things to find you. In Chapter Three, we looked briefly at the story in Luke 5 where Jesus had borrowed Peter's boat to teach the people who were gathered on the shore. When Jesus was finished, He wanted to pay Peter. He told him to launch out into the deep water and let down the nets for a catch of fish. Peter had just fished all night and caught nothing. As a professional fisherman, Peter knew the morning was not a good time to fish. He didn't feel like going back out and thought it would be a waste of his time. But instead of talking himself out of it, he said to Jesus, "Nevertheless, at Your word, I will do it." He chose to obey. When he threw out his nets, he caught so many fish that the nets began to break. He had to call over another boat to help him gather up all the fish.

> *Instead of talking himself out of it, he said to Jesus, "Nevertheless, at Your word, I will do it."*

That's what happens when you walk in obedience. There is a commanded blessing on your life. God will make things happen that you couldn't make happen. What's interesting is that there were no fish there during the night, but God controls the fish. He knows how to bring things to you even when conditions are not favorable, when you don't know the right people, or when you've had the addiction a long time. Perhaps no one in your family has really been successful. It looks as though that's the way it's always going to be for you. No, God is about to do a new thing. You tried and it didn't work out last time, but because of your obedience, God is speaking to the fish right now. It's not going to be a little catch, a little break, a little blessing. God's about to do something big, something so unusual that other people take notice. They will wonder, *What is it about you? How could you lead the company in sales? How could you beat the cancer? I saw the medical report. How could you marry that beautiful girl? How could you start your own business? That doesn't seem possible.* That's the commanded blessing. That's God causing the fish to find you. You may not see how this can happen, but neither did Peter. Everything in his reasoning said, "There are no fish out there."

In other words, it may be true that the medical report is not good, or that you've been single a long time, or that you don't have the training. The good news is, God is not limited by what you don't have, by who you don't know, or by the economy. All He has to do is speak and the fish will not only show up, they'll find you, they'll come to your boat. You don't have to make this happen, just keep God first place and let down your nets. This commanded blessing, like a magnet, will draw in good breaks, healing, favor, the right people.

More Than You Can Ask or Think

If you recall the previously told story of Ruth and Boaz, you see the commanded blessing in full display. Ruth would go out into Boaz's fields every morning and pick up the leftover wheat that the harvesters missed. She and her mother-in-law, Naomi, were living off scraps, barely able to survive. It didn't look as though there was a commanded blessing on Ruth's life. It didn't look as if their situation would ever change. Boaz could've said, "Tell the foreigner to get off my property. This is private land." Or he could've just not bothered with her at all, and that would have been the end. But when God caused Ruth to find favor with Boaz, what followed was one commanded blessing after another. She suddenly had so much wheat, more than she and Naomi needed. Not only that, she ended up falling in love with Boaz and they married. She went from working in the field to owning the field.

> *She went from working in the field to owning the field.*

When you have this commanded blessing on your life, God will cause you to find favor with the right people. You don't have to play up to people. You don't have to try to manipulate someone or convince them to like you. God will cause you to stand out as Ruth did. He'll bring divine connections, people who want to help you, not because of what you can do for them, not because of your training, your expertise, your looks, or your talents, but simply because God has caused them to show you favor.

Ruth couldn't have made this happen. She didn't know Boaz. She was a stranger in a foreign land, a poor widow. Nothing in her circumstances said she would ever be blessed, successful, owning those fields. When she first arrived at Bethlehem, if you had told her what was going to happen, she would've said, "That's impossible. There's no way." When you look at your circumstances, your dreams, the challenges you're facing, you may think it could never work out. Like Peter, you fished all night, and it didn't happen last time. Or maybe like Ruth, you've had some disappointments and setbacks. You're not where you thought you would be in life, but God knows how to not only bring the fish and the provision, but as with Ruth, he's going to bring the right people, people who will use their influence to help you go to the next level. If you could see where God is going to take you, the people He's going to bring, the doors He's going to open, and the influence He's going to give you, it would boggle your mind. You're going to look back and say, "I didn't see this coming. I didn't see owning the field coming. I didn't see the Compaq Center coming. I didn't see the healing, the freedom, the abundance." It's going to be more than you can ask or think.

The Commanded Blessing Is Yours

This is what happened to a friend of mine. He moved to Houston fourteen years ago with a dream to pursue starting his own business. He didn't know anyone here, didn't have any contacts, but he took a step of faith. He arrived in Houston on a Friday and on Sunday came to Lakewood. A month later, he was volunteering as an usher, serving in different ministries, honoring God, being his best. He started his business in the financial industry, and doors began to open. He had challenges and obstacles, but along the way he could see the hand of God. Then two years ago he was consulting with some clients in Chicago. He met an older gentleman who owned a huge financial firm, one of the largest in the world. This older man took an interest in him, started encouraging him and giving him advice. When this young man told him his vision—which all his critics had told him was too big and that he could never accomplish it—this man laughed and said, "Don't believe them. It's way too small. You're going to do something much bigger." The man had a desire to buy a part of this young man's company and came up with a valuation based on what the company would be worth in the future, far exceeding what it's worth today. My friend recently sold 25 percent of his company to this older gentleman, and now my friend owns one of the largest independent financial firms in all of Texas. What's interesting is that fourteen years ago he was stocking shelves in a grocery store to pay his rent. If you were to ask him, he would tell you, "I didn't see this coming. I never dreamed my business would take off. I never dreamed this man would be so good to me. I never dreamed I would be a leader in my field."

That's the commanded blessing. You keep honoring God, and He'll bring the right people. That older man didn't have to be good to him. He didn't have to value the company the way he did. He could've negotiated the price the other way. But God will cause people to want to be good to you. You may not think you know the right people, that you don't have the connections. Don't worry. God does. You keep honoring Him, and He's going to cause the right people to find you. He's going to open the right doors. He's going to bring the fish to your nets. One day you'll look back and say, "Wow! I didn't see that coming." It's because you've been commanded to be blessed.

He's going to bring the fish to your nets.

But sometimes we live as though we're commanded to struggle, commanded to be lonely, commanded to be addicted. Change has to take place inside, in our thinking, before it happens on the outside. Why don't you get rid of all the negative thoughts and start believing you're commanded to be blessed, commanded to be healthy, commanded to be free? If you do this, I believe and declare that as God did for my friend, He's about to command increase, command abundance, command healing, command freedom upon you.

CHAPTER THIRTEEN

Exceeded Expectations

We all have things that we're believing for, dreams to come to pass, problems to turn around. We'd be happy if they worked out our way, but sometimes what we have in mind is not God's best. We think ordinary; God thinks extraordinary. We think, *Let me have enough to get by*; God thinks abundance. We think, *Let me manage this addiction*; God thinks freedom. We're asking for the possible when God wants to do the impossible. He specializes in exceeding our expectations. What He has in store for you is bigger, more rewarding, more fulfilling than you can imagine.

The apostle Paul said in Ephesians 3 that God is able to do exceedingly abundantly above all we can ask or think. He's not just going to do what you're asking for, He's going to exceed it. He's going to open doors you never dreamed would open. He's going to take you further than you can imagine. You're going to look back and think, *I never dreamed I'd be this blessed, never dreamed I'd have this position, never dreamed I'd marry somebody this great.* Get ready. God is about to exceed your expectations. He's going to make things happen that you didn't see coming. You didn't deserve it, and you didn't work for it. It's just the goodness of God showing favor on your life.

"I Never Dreamed" Blessings

In Chapter Ten, I described the story of the crippled man in Acts 3 who sat outside the temple gate begging for money. He had done this his whole life, day after day. Here and there people would give him some coins. This is how he survived. When Peter and John walked past him that day, the man went through his same speech, "Can you spare some change? Will you help me out?" Most people ignored him and kept walking, but Peter stopped and said to the man, "Look at us." The Scripture says the man looked up expecting to receive a gift. I can see him holding his hand out for some coins, but Peter said, "I don't have any silver or gold for you, but I have something better. In the name of Jesus rise and walk." Peter took him by the hand, pulled him up, and instantly he was healed. He started walking and leaping and thanking God.

But notice what the man was expecting. He was expecting the ordinary, a few coins, the same thing that had happened the last forty years. But God showed up and exceeded his expectations. The man didn't see it coming. He thought he would have to lie by that gate and beg for the rest of his life, but one moment of favor, one exceeded expectation, thrust him to a new level and changed his whole life. I can hear him saying, "I never dreamed I'd be able to walk. I never dreamed I could run and play with my children. I never dreamed I wouldn't have to beg the rest of my life."

> *One moment of favor, one exceeded expectation, thrust him to a new level and changed his whole life.*

God has some of these "I never dreamed" blessings in store for you. You may not see how it can happen. The medical report doesn't look good. You've gone as far as your education allows, perhaps you're in a limited environment. The good news is, none of that stops our God. He controls the universe. One touch of His favor will catapult you where you could not go on your own. As Peter told the crippled man, I'm telling you to rise up and walk. It's your time to be free. It's your time to break bondages. It's your time to go to new levels. I believe that every force that's holding you back is being broken right now. God is releasing healing, favor, opportunities, restoration, and freedom. This is a new day. God's doing a new thing. He's about to exceed your expectations.

Astonishing

I love the fact that even though this crippled man had low expectations, even though all he was expecting was a few coins, God didn't say, "Too bad. I had something much better, but you don't have enough faith. I was going to bring you healing, but you're not expecting enough." God is so merciful. Even when we don't have the faith, even when we think we've reached our limits, God says, "That's okay. I'm going to show you favor in spite of that."

The Scripture says when we have faith the size of a mustard seed, nothing is impossible. A mustard seed is one of the smallest seeds. God could have said, "If you have great faith, if you never doubt and never get discouraged, I'll do something big." But God knows there will be times when we don't have the faith we need to reach our destinies, so He says, "If you have just a little bit of faith, that's all you need. Then I'll show up and exceed your expectations." The fact that you're reading this tells me you at least have mustard seed faith. That means you have the faith you need for God to show out in your life. You have the faith for God to catapult you to new levels, but, as with this man, you may feel that you're stuck, doing the same thing. You have some kind of disadvantage. Now you're expecting a few coins, so to speak, expecting the ordinary. That's where that man was, yet God showed up and did the extraordinary. You may have a good reason to settle where you are, but God loves you too much to let you miss your destiny. It may seem like just another ordinary day, the same old thing, everything looks

> *It may seem like just another ordinary day, the same old thing, everything looks routine. No, get ready.*

routine. No, get ready. God is about to show up and do something unusual, something that you haven't seen. He's going to exceed your expectation.

When the people in the temple saw the crippled man now healed, the Scripture says they were "astonished." What God is about to do in your life is going to cause people to look at you in astonishment. They're going to say, "How could you be so blessed? I know where you came from." "How could you be free when so many around you are addicted?" "How could you be so strong, so healthy, so energetic? The medical report said you weren't going to get well." God is going to make you an example of His goodness. When He exceeds your expectations, people are going to take notice. They're going to see the favor on your life.

Greater Than You've Imagined

When I look back over my life, I can see time and time again where God exceeded my expectations. I was twenty-two years old and single when I walked into a jewelry store to buy a battery for my watch. Out walked the most beautiful girl I'd ever seen to wait on me. It was Victoria. I had never met her. She looked at my watch and said, "You need more than a battery. You need a new watch. Would you like to see one?" I said, "Of course I would." I was so smitten with her that she could have sold me an electrical plant. She put that watch on my wrist and said, "That looks really nice."

Then she checked the price and said, "It's listed for this amount, but I can sell it to you for half price." Do you see how badly she wanted me? I went in there expecting to buy a battery for my watch, and in a sense I walked out not only with a new watch, but with a wife, with two children—with more than I could ask or think. Victoria is an exceeded expectation, and I remind her that she got me for a bargain, for half price.

I would love to tell you that I believed for all the increase, the favor, the promotion, and that the Compaq Center was all my idea because I had great faith. That's not the case. The Compaq Center wasn't my idea. It was God exceeding our expectations. I grew up with season tickets, watching the Houston Rockets play basketball in that auditorium. Never in my wildest dreams would I have thought that one day we would own this facility, and if you ever think that God can't exceed expectations, just give Lakewood a visit some time and look around. It is literally an exceeded expectation. "Well, Joel, I don't have great faith." Neither did I. "All the odds are against me." That's the same thinking as the crippled man's. None of that stops our God. When He exceeds your expectations, it's not going to be a little exceeded, a little more than you thought, a little blessing, a little increase. God is going to exceed it abundantly above what you're thinking. His idea of abundance is more than we can ask or think.

In 2004, when my first book was getting ready to go to press, I found out the publisher was going to print 250,000 copies. I couldn't believe it. I called Victoria and said, "The publisher must have lost their minds. They're making a huge mistake." My father would sell about 10,000 copies of each of his books. I was basing my expectations on that, but God doesn't want you to stay at the same level as your parents. He wants you to set a new standard. He's going to exceed your expectations in greater ways than how you were raised. As that crippled man did, I was expecting the ordinary, I was expecting the way I had grown up, but God showed up and did the extraordinary. He exceeded my expectations in an abundant way. That book went on to sell millions of copies.

Here is what I'm saying: What God has in store for you is much greater than you've imagined, and I believe sooner than later you're going to come into some of these exceeded expectations. Why don't you put your faith out there? Instead of thinking, *Oh, it's not going to happen for me, Joel, you're just trying to get my hopes up*, remember that you can't have faith if you don't first

> Why don't you put your faith out there?

have hope. Give God something to work with. Dare to say, "Lord, thank You that You're going to exceed my expectations. Thank You that You're going to take me where I could not go on my own."

The Right Breaks, the Right People

I heard about a man who had kidney problems most of his life. His condition continued to go downhill, and he got to the place where he needed a transplant. His wife prayed and believed that she would be a match. She was tested and learned she was a perfect match. They were both so grateful. They went to the Mayo Clinic to have the transplant. When the surgeons performed the procedure to remove one of the wife's kidneys, they were pleasantly surprised. They found she had three kidneys instead of two. This is very rare, but all of her kidneys were perfectly healthy. They removed one kidney, gave it to her husband, which still left her with two.

That was God exceeding their expectations. God has it all figured out. He knows what you're going to need. He knows who you're going to need. He's lining up the right breaks, the right people. He's directing your steps. Paul wrote in Ephesians about the surpassing greatness of God's favor. You're going to come into these moments where you see God surpass anything you've imagined. You couldn't have made it happen. It's just the goodness of God.

I have a minister friend who spends most of her time on the streets helping women who have been victims of abuse and are struggling with addictions. A while ago, through a series of unusual events, she met one of the wealthiest men in the world. He asked her what she did for a living. She explained how she helps women in crisis. He said, "That's amazing. I want to support you." He gave her the largest check she had ever received. As she was leaving his office, this man's friend came walking in. He said to his friend, "This woman helps ladies who are in trouble. I just gave her a gift. How much are you going to give?" Without missing a beat, the friend said, "I'm going to give the same amount that you just gave." This lady walked out amazed, thinking, *I never dreamed I would have two of the wealthiest men in the world supporting my ministry.* What was that? God doing more than she could ask or think. You may wonder how you're going to accomplish your dreams or how you're going to get out of that difficulty. God has the right people lined up. He knows how to put you at the right place. He's going to make things happen that you didn't see coming.

Pass the Test

I woke up one morning and heard this phrase so strong in my spirit: "God is going to exceed our expectations." Victoria and I were out of town in another state at the time. We had been trying to get a project off the ground for several months with no success, one closed door after another, and we'd not been able to connect with the right person. When I heard that phrase, I started saying it: "Lord, thank You that You're going to exceed my expectations." I kept that playing in my mind over and over. Later that day we were about to catch a flight home, and Victoria said, "Let's run back to the one business place and give this one last try." We went to the business, but the doors were locked because it was a holiday. We needed someone to help us, so we called the number listed on the outside door. A man answered our call and said, "I was expecting a call from someone else. I thought

this was their number, otherwise I wouldn't have answered it."
When we told him what we wanted, he responded, "I'm out
with my family, but I want to help you. I'll be right over."

He came to where we were, and our
project all came together. We were
at the right place at the right time
with the right person. In less than
twenty-four hours the whole thing
was finished. It was much better
than we expected, and it happened
much more quickly than we ever dreamed.

> *It was much better
> than we expected, and
> it happened much
> more quickly than we
> ever dreamed.*

But I believe that when I heard that phrase that morning, it was a test. Was I going to let that seed take root
and believe that God could exceed my expectations, or was
I going to dismiss it and think, *Oh, that's a nice thought,
but it will never happen?*

God is saying to you today, "I'm about to exceed your
expectations. I'm about to show you favor in ways that you've
never seen." My challenge is: Let this take root in your
spirit. It's easy to dismiss it and say, "It will never happen.
The odds are against me. It's been too long."

This is exactly what happened to the Shunammite lady we
looked at in Chapter Eleven. She and her husband had tried
for many years to have a baby, and she had accepted that it
just wasn't meant to be. When the prophet Elisha told her,
"By this time next year you're going to have a child," she
heard his words in the natural and thought, *That's impossible.
My husband is too old. I'm past the childbearing years. There's*

no way. Deep down she wanted to believe, but her mind told her all the reasons why it wasn't going to happen. She said to Elisha, "Sir, don't lie to me like that." She was saying, in effect, "Don't get my hopes up. That's too good to be true." This was a dream that was so close to her heart. She wanted it so badly, but she just didn't have the faith. The good news is, there are some things that, even if you don't believe, God is still going to do them for you. He is so merciful that He will override the doubt and do things you never dreamed, things that will bring you more joy, more fulfillment than you can imagine. God exceeded her expectations even though she didn't believe. That's the kind of God we serve.

There are promises God has spoken over you, dreams He's put in your heart. It seems impossible. It's been so long. You're not expecting it anymore. God is saying to you what He said to her: "I'm still going to bring it to pass." Just because you gave up doesn't mean God has given up, and I believe, as with her, some of these things you're going to see by this time next year. You may not see a way, but God has a way. If this lady didn't believe and saw the promise fulfilled, imagine what God will do when you do believe. Put your faith out there.

More Than You Asked

"But, Joel, I've been doing this for a long time, a lot more than a year. Nothing is changing. I don't see anything happening."

That means you're right where a woman named Hannah was in the book of 1 Samuel. She had been married for many years, but she, too, was barren. Her husband had a second wife who had baby after baby and would make fun of Hannah and taunt her that she was unable to have children. This went on year after year. The husband tried to comfort Hannah, saying, "Don't worry about her. I love you," but none of this helped. Hannah was so distraught, so upset. She knew God put the dream in her heart. She couldn't understand why it wasn't happening.

One day Hannah went to the temple and fell on the ground. In great distress she called out to God and said, "God, if You give me a son, I'll give him back to You. I'll bring him to the temple and let him live there." When Eli the priest saw her on the ground crying, he came over and said, "Hannah, cheer up. The Lord has heard your request. He's going to give you a son. Go in peace." She received that promise in her spirit, and she conceived. Nine months later she gave birth to a baby boy whom she named Samuel. She was so content. She had the child she had dreamed about, and this could have been the great end to the story, another promise fulfilled, but God likes to exceed our expectation. The Scripture says the Lord visited Hannah again, and she bore three more sons and two daughters. She asked for one son, but notice how good our

> *"You may be satisfied, but I'm not satisfied. I'm going to do more than you asked."*

God is. He said, in effect, "Hannah, you may be satisfied, but I'm not satisfied. I'm going to do more than you asked."

I believe that one reason God was so good to Hannah was because of all the pain she had endured, having to wait while the other wife was having babies, being made fun of, ridiculed. God sees all the heartache, all the tears, the unfair situations, the people who did you wrong. What you're believing for may not have happened yet, it may be taking a long time as with Hannah, but God is faithful. He's not only still going to bring it to pass—that would be good enough, you would be satisfied—but God is going to do more than you've asked. That means once you have your baby, so to speak, once you see the promise fulfilled, God is not finished being good to you. He's going to visit you again. He's going to show out in another way. You asked for one baby, and God has five more waiting for you. He's going to pay you back for what you've been through. Our attitude should be, *Lord, thank You that You're going to visit me again. Thank You that You're going to do more than I ask. Thank You for exceeding my expectations.*

Increased, Promoted, Stronger

In 2 Chronicles 20, King Jehoshaphat was surrounded by three major armies described as "a great multitude." Jehoshaphat called everyone together to pray. He said, "God, we have no power against this mighty army without Your help. We do not know what to do, but our eyes are on You. Please deliver us." God said to the king, "Don't be afraid. The battle is not yours. The battle is the Lord's. Tomorrow march toward the enemies, but you will not need to fight. Stand still, and you will see the Lord deliver you." They were excited. They had the promise that God was going to fight for them, and as they marched toward those enemies the next day, they started singing, thanking God. When the enemies heard all the noise, the commotion, they got confused and started fighting among themselves. They ended up killing one another—no one escaped. When the people of Judah showed up, not only did they not have to fight, but all the supplies of the enemy were left there. The Scripture says they found vast amounts of equipment, clothing, and other valuables, more than they could carry. It took them three days to gather up the spoils and take them back to their homes.

Jehoshaphat asked for God to deliver them from those enemies, and God did. They didn't even have to fight. That was a great miracle, something worth celebrating. The king could have gone back home thanking God, so grateful, but our God exceeds our expectations. As with Hannah, He said, in effect, "Jehoshaphat, I'm going to visit you again. I'm not going to do just what you asked, I'm not going to just bring you out, but I'm going to make the enemy pay. I'm going to bring you out increased, promoted, and stronger." They marched toward those enemies empty-handed, and they came back loaded down with supplies. You may have obstacles in your path and challenges coming against you today in your health, your finances, or a relationship. You're asking God to turn it around. Stay encouraged. God is not only going to bring you out, He's going to have some spoils there. There is going to be some plunder. He's going to bring you out better than you were before. He's going to exceed your expectations.

> *There is going to be some plunder. He's going to bring you out better than you were before.*

Now don't talk yourself out of it. Sometimes when we've struggled in an area for a long time, we've gotten comfortable. As with the crippled man, we're expecting a few coins, something to sustain us, to help us make it through. God is about to do a new thing. You're asking for the possible; He's about to do the impossible. He's going to take you where you've never been. No more coins, no more dysfunction, no more being barren, no more stuck in your career. You're about to come into some of these exceeded expectations. God is going to do more than you've asked. You've been faithful, you've honored Him; now God is about to show out in your life. Every morning say, "Lord, thank You that You're going to exceed my expectations." If you do this, I believe and declare that God is about to visit you again. He's been good to you, you've had your Samuel, but you haven't seen anything yet. New doors are about to open, increase, promotion that you didn't see coming. Problems are turning around, health is being restored, exceeded expectations are coming your way!

CHAPTER FOURTEEN

It's on the Way

What you're believing for, the promises you're standing on, the dreams you've been praying about, they're already en route. The healing is coming, the promotion is coming, the favor is coming, the right people are coming. You may not see any signs of it yet; everything looks the same. What you can't see is that behind the scenes, God is moving the wrong people out of the way, pushing back the forces of darkness. He's arranging things in your favor, lining up the breaks you need. He's called the Author and the Finisher of our faith. He's going to finish what He started in your life. God didn't bring you this far to leave you. You may have big challenges, but we serve a big God. Your enemies may be powerful, but our God is all-powerful. That dream may look impossible. You don't think you have the connections, the resources, or the talent, but God can do the impossible. Even when the odds are against you, God is for you, and He's saying, "Favor is on the way."

Sometimes you need these words of faith spoken over

your life. Words have creative power. If you let them take
root, they'll ignite the faith in your spirit. Because life has
a way of pushing us down, if you're not careful, you will
look up and realize that you're not believing as you once
did. You're not passionate, not dreaming. You don't see how
your situation could ever work out. But here's the key: You
don't have to figure it out. Our job is to believe. Our job
is to go out each day with expectancy and say, "God, I
may not see a way, but I know You have a way. I believe
my breakthrough is on the way. I believe my healing, the
promotion, freedom from this addiction—it's just a matter of
time before it shows up." If you don't have this anticipation
that it's on the way, it can keep it from happening.

You may have big obstacles in your path that you can't
overcome on your own. The good news is, you're not on
your own. You have the most power-

> *You have the most
> powerful force in the
> universe breathing in
> your direction.*

ful force in the universe breathing
in your direction. When He speaks,
Red Seas part, blind eyes open,
dreams come back to life. We look
at our circumstances in the natural,
but He's a supernatural God. The prophet Isaiah says that
He's going before you, making your crooked places straight,
fighting your battles. No person can stop you—no bad break,
no sickness, no failure. Get your fire back. You have to stir
up your faith. Maybe at one time you believed, you were
passionate and excited about life, but things haven't turned
out the way you hoped. You had some bad breaks, some

disappointments. God is saying, "It's time to believe again. It's time to dream again." You haven't seen your best days. What God promised you is still going to come to pass. It's not too late. You haven't missed too many opportunities. If it had happened sooner, it wouldn't have been the right time. Now is the time. Start believing again.

It's Not Dead; It's Just Asleep

Maybe somebody walked out on you in the past, somebody did you wrong, but that didn't stop God's plan for you. Don't give up on your dreams and live hurt and wounded, thinking they ruined your life. They don't control your destiny. They don't have that much power over you. What they did may not have been fair, but God is going to make it up to you. He's saying new beginnings are on the way—new friendships, new opportunities. They meant it for your harm, but God's going to use it for your good. The problem you're facing is not too big for our God. The medical report is not too bad, because He has the final say. He says that healing is on the way. He's going to restore health back to you. You may have struggled in your finances for a long time; you can't seem to get ahead. Now you've just settled there, thinking that's the way it's always going to be. God is saying, "I have increase on the way. I have favor, promotion, and opportunities that have your name on them." God says He will open the windows of Heaven and pour out blessings that we cannot contain. Why don't you get up each day and say, "Father, thank You that abundance is coming my way. Thank You that I'll lend and not borrow. Thank You that You're opening doors that no man can shut." When you live with this expectancy, that's when dreams come to pass, doors open that you could never open. That's when you'll see explosive blessings that catapult you to the next level.

But too many people have given up on what God put in their heart. They tried and it didn't work out; now they think the dream is dead. They'll never get well, never meet the right person, never come into abundance. But what you think is dead is not really dead. That seed is still alive. God doesn't abort dreams. He doesn't give up on what He put in us.

In John 11, word came to Jesus that his good friend Lazarus was very sick. He was in another city, and they asked Jesus to come pray for him. Jesus was delayed for a couple days, and Lazarus died. But it's interesting that Jesus said to His disciples, "Our friend Lazarus has fallen asleep. I am going there to wake him up." Lazarus was clearly dead, but Jesus had a different perspective. He said Lazarus was only asleep. Could it be what you think is dead really isn't dead? Perhaps you think your marriage is never going to make it, or you'll never get well, or you'll never accomplish the dream. As Lazarus was in the grave, all the circumstances say that it's over and done, but God says, "I have a different perspective. I can see things that you can't see. It's not dead; it's just asleep." It may look permanent, but the truth is, it's only temporary.

Jesus showed up at Lazarus's house four days late. Lazarus had been in the tomb so long that he stunk. His body was so dead that it smelled bad. At times, we all have things in life that stink. Maybe your marriage feels so dead that it stinks. That bankruptcy stinks. That layoff stinks. That mistake you made that set you back stinks. Jesus went to the tomb and told them to roll away the stone. Martha said, "No, Jesus. It smells too bad. You're not going to like it. You're going to be put off by it." Jesus said, "No, Martha. Have them roll away that stone."

What's the point? Jesus went to where the stink was. Sometimes we think that God will only help us if we've lived perfectly, if everything is nice and whole, but God goes to the stinky places in our lives. That person who hurt you, did you wrong, it stinks. God is saying, "Let Me in. I'm going to wake up the healing, wake up the restoration, wake up the new beginning." That mistake you made, you feel condemned, every voice tells you, "God's not going to bless you. Nothing good is coming your way. You blew it. You stink." God is saying, "No. Roll that stone away. I'm not bothered by the stink." God goes to the stinky places where you were betrayed, where you lost the loved one, where you compromised, where you feel disqualified. God says, "Let Me in. The stink is only temporary. The dream is not dead; it's just asleep."

Jesus looked into the tomb at Lazarus and called out in a loud voice, "Lazarus, come forth!" Lazarus woke up. He'd been dead for four days, but he came out of the tomb and went on to live for many more years. I believe that things you've given up on, things that you think are dead, like Lazarus, they're about to wake up. Marriages are waking up, dreams are waking up, healing is waking up, abundance is waking up. God is saying to us what He said to the disciples, "It's not dead; it's just asleep. Healing is coming, joy is coming, victory is coming." It may have been asleep for a long time. You think, *There's no way it could happen now*. That's what Mary and Martha thought. But it's not too late, it's not too far gone. You need to get ready. God's about to wake it up.

Wake Up the Dream

This is what God did for Sarah in the Scripture. She and her husband, Abraham, had tried for decades to have a baby. When Sarah was eighty years old, everything logically speaking said there's no way it could happen, but God promised them she would bear a son. What God has promised you, He's still going to bring to pass. He's not limited by the laws of nature. You are not at the mercy of your age, your education, or your background.

> *God has unlimited power. One touch of His favor can turn a situation around.*

God has unlimited power. One touch of His favor can turn a situation around. Sarah thought her womb was dead; she didn't realize that it was only asleep. At ninety-one years old, she gave birth to a baby; the promise came to pass.

God has put dreams and promises in you as He did in Sarah. It may not have happened yet. You tried again and again, and it didn't work out. Now maybe you've settled there and think, *Well, it's just not meant to be*, but God is full of surprises. He's about to wake up that dream you've given up on. He's about to bring to life what you thought was dead. Your latter days are going to be more rewarding, more fulfilling, than your former days. You're going to give birth to more in the future than you've lost in the past. Your baby is on the way, your promise is on the way, that dream is on the way.

As a young man, Moses made a mistake and killed a man. He was trying to deliver God's people from Egypt, he had that dream in his heart, but he got into a hurry. He had to flee for his life. He ended up spending years on the backside of the desert. I'm sure he thought, *I had a big dream. I knew I was going to do something great with my life. I knew I was going to leave my mark, but I blew it.* He gave up on his dream. He had nobody to blame except himself. But just because we give up doesn't mean God gives up. Forty years later, God came to him and said, "Moses, I'm here to wake up your dream. Now it's time to go deliver My people." Moses went out and did just that. He saw his dream come to pass.

As Moses did, you may have made mistakes; we all have. As Sarah had, you may have had disappointments; your plans didn't work out and now you think it's been too long. What you've given up on is not dead; it's just asleep. That business you wanted to start, that book you wanted to write, that addiction you've been trying to break—every thought tells you, "It's too late. You're too old. It's never going to happen." No, get ready. God's about to wake it up. Your baby is coming, your spouse is coming, that business is coming, the freedom is coming. Now get in agreement with God. He's waking it up, so don't let it go back to sleep. Stir up your faith. Believe that it's on the way. Go out with expectancy. When your mind tells you, "You're never going to get well," wake up the healing. "God is restoring health back to me." When it says, "You'll never get out of debt," wake up the abundance. "I will lend and not borrow." When it tells you, "You'll never overcome that problem," wake up the victory. "God always causes me to triumph." Keep your mind going in the right direction.

Marvelous Faith

In Mark 6, Jesus went back to his hometown and began to teach the people in the synagogue. They had heard that Jesus had done great miracles, calmed the seas, opened blind eyes. But when they saw Him up there teaching, they thought, *That's just Jesus. We grew up with him. That's the carpenter's son. There's nothing special about him.* Because they didn't believe in Him, He couldn't do many miracles in His hometown. The Scripture says, "Jesus marveled at their unbelief." By way of contrast, in the book of Matthew, a Roman officer came to Jesus and said, "One of my employees is very sick. You don't need to come to my house. Just speak the word, and I know he'll be healed." When Jesus heard this, the Scripture says, "He was amazed and said, 'I have not found such great faith in all of Israel.'" In one place, Jesus marveled at their doubt, and in the other, He marveled at their faith.

When God looks at you, what will He marvel at? "I'll never get well, Joel. I've had this sickness so long. I'll never accomplish my dreams. I tried, and it didn't work out." When you think like that, God marvels at your unbelief. That ties His hands. Why don't you come over into faith? "Yes, I've had this sickness a long time, but I know my healing is on the way. I had a bad break, it wasn't fair, but I know God has beauty for these ashes. I know favor is in my future." When we think like that, God marvels at your faith. That's what allows Him to do more than we can ask or think.

What's interesting is that the people who doubted, the people who had the unbelief, were the religious people. They were in the synagogue each week. They were the faithful members. I say this respectfully, but sometimes religion will try to talk you out of God's best. It will tell you, "In the sweet by-and-by you can live a victorious life, but down here you just have to suffer through it, just endure. Don't expect too much." If Jesus were here, He would marvel at that unbelief. My father was taught in seminary years ago that the day of miracles was over. "God doesn't still heal and bless and show favor. That was for Bible days." But we learned there never was a day of miracles; there's a God of miracles. He's still alive. He's still on the throne. My point is that this Roman officer who had great faith wasn't a religious person.

> *There never was a day of miracles; there's a God of miracles.*

He hadn't been indoctrinated to think that it couldn't happen. He simply believed, *That man is the Son of God. I've seen Him do miracles. He's done it for others, and He can do it for me.* He received his miracle while the religious people went without.

When you take the limits off God and dare to believe for your dreams, don't be surprised if people try to talk you out of it. They will say things such as, "You really think you'll get well? You really believe you can start that business? You're going to break that addiction? I don't know. Seems kind of far out to me." God's going to either marvel at your faith or marvel at your unbelief. Don't let another person talk you out of what God put in your heart. Believe big, dream big, and pray big. God is longing to be good to you. He wants to make you an example of His goodness so that everywhere you go, you don't even have to say anything—your life is a testimony. People will look at you and say, "He's blessed. She's highly favored." You radiate joy, peace, favor, and victory. You're a living testimony.

Jesus didn't say to the Roman officer, "I'm not going to do anything for you. You don't attend my synagogue. You don't come to my church." He didn't say, "You're not my nationality. You don't look like me. Who do you think you are?" None of that made any difference. All that mattered to Jesus was: "This man has great faith. He believes I can do something out of the ordinary, so I'm going to show myself strong in his life." You may think that you're not religious enough, so God would never help you. People tell me often, "Joel, I watch you, but I'm not a religious person. I wasn't raised in church like you." It's almost as though they're apologizing. Can I tell you, God is not looking for religion. He's looking for people who simply believe in Him, who know He controls the universe, who believe He can do the impossible.

The Only Possible Explanation

I received an email from a couple. Not long after they were married, the husband started having problems with his balance and muscle control. His muscles would tighten up so much at night that he could barely get out of bed in the morning. His wife had to help him get into the car and sometimes take him to work because he couldn't drive. This kept getting worse and worse. It got to where he could not pick up their baby daughter. They went to a doctor, and after many tests he was diagnosed with a progressive muscular disease that's incurable, something like muscular dystrophy. They were devastated. At night the thoughts came to the wife, *What if he can't work? What if you lose your job and you can't afford the house? What if he dies? Your daughter will grow up without a father.* They weren't raised in church and didn't have any religious background. But one night at three o'clock in the morning, while she was massaging his legs because they were in so much pain, they turned on the television and there was our program. As they listened, they heard about the favor and goodness of God and how God can do what medicine cannot do, and something ignited inside.

It just so happened that a few months later our Night of Hope event was coming to their city, and they attended. The man could barely make the long walk from the parking lot to the auditorium. At the end of the service, they both stood up and gave their lives to Christ. The wife said, "In an instant we knew our lives were changed forever. We could feel we were different inside." They started believing that healing was coming their way. Walking back from the auditorium to the car, she noticed that her husband was not in as much pain. As the weeks went by, the symptoms got less and less. Months later they came to Houston for their annual checkup with their same team of doctors. After they ran all the tests to get the new markers, the doctors came in looking baffled. They said, "We can't explain it. We've never seen this happen, but we can't find any sign of the disease." One of the doctors asked the man if there was anything he had done differently. He said, "The only thing that I've done differently is I gave my life to Christ." The doctor said, "That's the only explanation I can give you." As with the Roman officer, they weren't religious people, but they dared to believe. It looked impossible, but they said, "God, we know You can do the impossible. We believe healing is on the way."

In the Old Testament, the Israelites had wandered around in the desert for many years and God was about to take them into the Promised Land. But there were seven nations in their path that were much bigger. Moses didn't know what they were going to do. In the natural, they could never defeat them. But God said to them in Deuteronomy 7, "I'm going to go before you and clear out these seven nations that are stronger and more powerful than you." God is saying, "You don't have to fight these battles on your own strength. I'm going before you to clear the path. I'm going to make things happen you couldn't make happen. I'm going to defeat your enemies for you."

As was true for the Israelites, we all face times when the odds are against us. It's easy to think, *This incurable muscle disease, this sickness is much bigger than me. This addiction is much stronger than me. These people coming against me are much more powerful.* Don't worry. God is going before you right now clearing the path. On your own you may be outnumbered. What you're up against

> What you're up against may be bigger, stronger, more talented, and have more resources, but you're not on your own.

may be bigger, stronger, more talented, and have more resources, but you're not on your own. The God who controls the universe says He will take care of your enemies. In other words, the cancer may be stronger than you, but it's not stronger than our God. That debt may look insurmountable, you don't see how you could ever get out of it, but it's no match for our God. He owns it all. He makes streets out of gold.

Stand Still and See

I talked to a gentleman recently who's struggled with a drug addiction for many years. He's an executive, has a great position, and nobody knows about it. But the addiction is ruining his life. He said, "Joel, I feel powerless. I've tried everything. I can't stop." I told him what I'm telling you. On your own you can't, but you have the God who spoke worlds into existence on your side. Instead of saying, "I can't do it," and dwelling on the negative, all through the day say, "Father, thank You that You're defeating my enemies. Thank You that You're clearing the path. I know You're stronger than this addiction, more powerful than this cancer, bigger than this debt. Lord, thank You that healing is coming; wholeness, freedom, and victory are on the way." The Scripture puts it this way: "It's not by our might, not by our power, but by the Spirit of the Most High God." You don't have to do it on your own.

When Pharaoh and his army seemed to have the Israelites trapped at the Red Sea, Moses told them, "Stand still, and you will see the deliverance of the Lord." You may be up against something big right now. Don't get discouraged, don't live stressed out, just stand still. God is clearing the path. He is fighting your battles. He's going to give you victory over powerful enemies. It may not happen overnight, but as long as you're believing, God is at work. At the right time He's going to take you into your Promised Land. That victory is on the way.

A young lady we know was seventy-five thousand dollars in debt from her college education. She's in her twenties, just getting started in her career. That debt looked so much bigger, so much stronger than her. In the natural, she would be paying on it for years to come. But she heard me speak about how God wants to accelerate things, how He can make it happen faster than we think. She dared to believe that word was for her. She let the seed take root. Something told her to call the school and see if there was any way they could help. They sent her an application to get assistance with the debt. She filled it out and sent

> *She dared to believe that word was for her. She let the seed take root.*

it back to them. A couple days later they called her back and said, "Your application has been approved. We've decided to forgive the whole seventy-five-thousand-dollar debt." God can make things happen that we could never make happen. Right now He's going before you, defeating enemies that are much more powerful. That debt may look as if it's going to be with you your whole life, but get ready. As God did for her, He's clearing the path. That sickness, that addiction, that legal problem may be bigger, stronger, and more powerful, but it's no match for our God. He is all-powerful.

I'm asking you to stir up your faith. Don't read all of this and be like the people in Jesus' hometown, where He marveled at the unbelief. Let's have the Roman officer's belief, where He marvels at our faith. Those dreams you've given up on, those promises you've let go of—you need to get them back. They're not dead; they're just asleep. As with Lazarus, God is about to wake up what you thought was over and done. I believe and declare healing is on the way, freedom is on the way, God's favor is on the way. Abundance is on the way!

CHAPTER FIFTEEN

Living Favor-Minded

God told Abraham, "I will bless you with an abundant increase of favors." He did not mean just one or two favors. He said, "I'm going to do favors for you in abundance." You and I are the seed of Abraham. What would happen if we really believed that the Creator of the universe wants to do favors for us?

Most of the time we think, *God has bigger things to deal with than me. He's not interested in that.* No, you are God's biggest deal. He wants to make you an example of His goodness. The word *favor* means "to assist, to provide with advantages, to receive preferential treatment." The favor of God will cause you to be promoted even though you aren't the most qualified. God's favor will cause your children to get the best teachers in school. It will help you find the best deals at the mall. It will put you at the right place at the right time. God is saying to you what He said to Abraham: "I'm going to assist you. I'm going to provide you with advantages. I'm going to cause you to receive preferential treatment."

"Well, Joel, this never happens for me. I must not have this favor." No, you have it, but the reason many people don't experience it is that they're not releasing their faith in this area. They're not expecting good breaks. They don't expect preferential treatment. They have an underdog mentality. They say, "Everybody gets promoted except me." "I put my house on the market. I should have known it wouldn't sell." "I went to the grocery store and got in the longest line. Just my luck."

If you're going to experience this favor, you have to live favor-minded. That means you're expecting it and you're declaring it. Every day before you leave the house you should say, "Father, thank You that I have Your favor." Then go out expecting good things to happen. Expect doors to open for you that may not open for somebody else. You have an advantage. There is something special about you. You have the favor of God. I'm not talking about being arrogant and thinking that we're better than somebody else. I'm talking about living with boldness—not because of who we are but because of Whose we are. You are a child of the Most High God. Your Father created the whole universe. You can expect preferential treatment.

> *Expect doors to open for you that may not open for somebody else.*

Your Father Owns It All

If you were born into the Rockefeller family, you're going to have some advantages. If you were born into the Kennedy family or Bill Gates' family, you're going to be treated differently. You're going to expect favor that other people may not expect. The good news today is, you have been born into the right family. You come from a royal bloodline. Your Father owns it all. You need to hold your head high and start expecting to stand out in the crowd. Start expecting good breaks, divine connections, and opportunities to come your way. You have favor because of who your Father is.

As a young boy, I received preferential treatment because of my earthly father. We used to travel with my dad during the summers when he would speak at large conferences. One time when I was ten years old, we were in the lobby of a big hotel in Chicago. My little sister, April, and I were standing at the coffee shop admiring the pictures of milkshakes for sale up on the overhead menu. An older lady came by and said, "Aren't you John Osteen's children?" I said with a smile, "Yes, ma'am. We are." She said, "How about I buy you one of those milkshakes you're looking at?" I thought about it for about two-tenths of a second and said, "That would be nice." She bought us a milkshake. It wasn't because of anything that I had done. She did me a favor simply because of who my father was. The rest of the week I hung out at that coffee shop!

I mentioned in Chapter Three that when I was nineteen years old, I got pulled over by a policeman for driving too fast. The officer was kind of gruff. He seemed like he was having a bad day. I was young and nervous. My heart was beating so fast. He came over to my window and I handed him my driver's license. He stared at it for the longest time. A minute or two went by. It seemed like forever. Then he finally looked at me and said, "Are you related to that uh... that uh..." He said it three times. "That uh... preacher?"

By the way he said it, I didn't know if it was going to be a good thing to be related to my father at that moment. I smiled and said, "It depends." He said, "What do you mean, it depends?" I said, "It depends on whether or not you like him." He looked up in the air as though he was trying to decide. I thought, *That's not a good sign if he has to think about it*. He looked at me and said, "Yeah, I watch him on television a lot. I kind of like him." I said, "Good, because he's my father. He sure wouldn't want you to give me a ticket." Believe it or not, he let me go. What was that? Preferential treatment because of who my father was.

> *Why don't you start carrying yourself like you're a child of the King?*

Why don't you start carrying yourself like you're a child of the King? Why don't you start expecting some advantages, some good breaks, even some preferential treatment? Instead of thinking, *Nobody likes me at work. I'll never get ahead*, start declaring, "I have the favor of God. People are drawn to me. People want to be good to me. People go out of their way to be nice." That's not just being positive; that's releasing your faith. If you're going to see an abundant increase of God's favors, you can't have a limited, short-end-of-the-stick, underdog mentality.

Crowned with Favor

It says in the Psalms that God has crowned you with His favor. You may not be able to see it, but everywhere you go you are wearing a crown on your head. That crown does not represent lack, bad breaks, mediocrity, or barely getting by. It represents the favor of God. It represents the fact that the Creator of the universe breathed His life into you. In the unseen realm, the spiritual world, all the forces of darkness can see that you are wearing your robe of righteousness. They can see your crown of favor on your head. That tells them that you've been set apart. They can see you have a right to preferential treatment. They can see there is something different about you. But here is the problem: If you don't see yourself the right way, it's going to limit you. When you need an advantage, a good break, instead of shrinking back and thinking, *Oh, what's the use? It's never going to happen,* stand tall and imagine that crown of favor on your head. Let that be a reminder that you have a right to live in victory. You have a right to stand out in the crowd. You have a right to these special advantages.

Through my eyes of faith I can see your crown of favor.

I see royalty. I see increase. I see new doors opening. I see problems turning around. I see dreams coming to pass. The enemy tells you, "You're never going to get promoted. Your boss doesn't even like you." "You're never going to take that missions trip. You don't have the connections." "You'll never pay off your house. Your salary isn't going up." Tell him, "Hang on just a minute. I have to fix something up here." He says, "What are you doing?" "I'm straightening my crown of favor. I'm making sure that it's on tight." You're not average. You're not ordinary. You come from a royal family. You can expect advantages that other people may not expect. God has crowned you with His favor.

I received a letter from a mother who was a single parent. She immigrated to the United States from Europe many years ago. English is not her first language. She had three small children and didn't know how she would ever be able to afford to send them to college. It seemed like she was at a disadvantage.

She applied for a job as a secretary at a prestigious university. Several dozen other people applied for the same position. When she saw all the competition, she was tempted to feel intimidated. Negative thoughts were bombarding her mind. To make matters worse, the lady conducting the interview was not nice to her. She was harsh and condescending. But this mother didn't get frustrated by it. She didn't have an underdog mentality, thinking, *What's the use? I'm at a disadvantage.* She knew she was wearing a crown of favor. She knew God could cause her to stand out in the crowd. The whole time she was saying under her breath, "Lord, thank You for Your favor."

All the applicants had to take a five-minute typing test. Typing was not her strength, but she started typing, doing her best. The bell went off signaling that her five minutes were up, so she stopped typing. But the lady in charge had gotten distracted by a phone call and said to her gruffly, "Keep typing! That's not your bell." But it was her bell. It was right in front of her. She said, "Okay," and typed for another five minutes. They added up the number of words she'd typed—ten minutes' worth—and divided it by five, and by far she appeared to have the best typing skills and ended up getting the job.

One of the benefits of working for this university was that her children got to go to school for free. That was over thirty years ago. Today, all three of her children have graduated from this very prestigious university, having received over $700,000 in education all free of charge. What was that? An abundant increase of favor.

God knows how to give you an advantage. He knows how to put you at the right place at the right time. Instead of thinking, *It's never going to happen. I always get the short end of the stick,* why don't you straighten your crown of favor? Why don't you start declaring, "The favor of God is opening the right doors for me. The favor of God is causing me to stand out. The favor of God is taking me where

I could not go on my own"? That's what it means to live favor-minded. You're expecting it, and you're declaring it.

Expect Special Advantages

I was at an airport ticket counter back in the 1990s. Victoria and I were headed to New Delhi, India, where my father was having a large pastors' conference. We were going over a few days early. I was hand-carrying a very expensive television camera that I didn't want to check into luggage. On previous flights I had taken it on board, but the lady at the counter was very opposed to that. She said, "Sir, you don't have a choice. Put it back in the case and check it like luggage."

I was very polite, but I explained to her that I really wanted to carry it on board to protect it, and that I had done it several times before, even on that same airline. She wasn't about to budge. I didn't get upset. I knew I had a secret weapon. While she continued to check us in, under my breath I started saying, "Lord, thank You that Your favor is giving me an advantage. Thank You that Your favor will cause me to have preferential treatment."

I asked her if there was anyone I could talk to about possibly making an exception. She said, "The only person who has that authority is the captain of the flight himself. He can't be bothered. He's getting prepared for the flight."

About that time a gentleman who was wearing a uniform walked up. He could see that we were discussing something and asked her what the problem was. She said, "He wants to take the camera on board, but he'll have to put it under his seat, and that will be awkward."

The man asked me what flight I was on. I said, "We're going to New Delhi." He said, "Oh! I'm the captain of that flight. You can put it in my compartment right behind the cockpit." That lady's eyes got as big as saucers. Out of thousands of people in the airport, what were the chances of that captain walking up right when I needed him? That wasn't a lucky break. It wasn't a coincidence. It was the favor of God giving me special advantages. God's favor will put the right people at the right place at the right time.

Maybe you need to get your crown of favor out. Dust it off and put it back on your head. You're not expecting these advantages. You need to start expecting good breaks. Start expecting people to want to help you. God wants to show you an abundant increase of His favors, but if you're not releasing your faith for it, it will limit what He can do.

> *God wants to show you an abundant increase of His favors.*

You can't reach your highest potential on your own. You need God's favor. You need Him to assist you, to provide you with advantages, to cause you to have preferential treatment. Don't be passive and think, *If God wants to bless me, He'll bless me. If He wants to give me a good break, He is God, and He can give me a good break.* God is moved by our faith. When you expect it and declare it, that's when the Creator of the universe can show up and do amazing things.

It takes a boldness to believe that Almighty God will do you favors. Every voice will tell you, "What are you talking about? God is not interested in you. You don't deserve it. Who do you think you are?" Just put your shoulders back and say, "I'm a child of the Most High God, and I'm crowned with His favor."

Think about how we as parents love to do favors for our children. How much more does God want to do favors for you, His child? My question is, Are you expecting it? Are you declaring it?

Favor Surrounds You

Psalm 5 says that God's favor surrounds us like a shield. If it surrounds us, it's with us everywhere we go. You have favor at work, favor at the grocery store, favor at the gym, favor in traffic, and favor at the mall. The more aware you are of this favor, the more conscious you are that God wants to assist you, the more you'll see His hand at work.

All through the day, even if it's under our breath, we should get in this habit of declaring, "Lord, thank You for Your favor. Thank You that I have favor with my boss and clients. Lord, thank You that my children have favor with their teachers and coaches." At the grocery store, be saying, "Lord, thank You that Your favor is helping me find what I need." In traffic, be saying, "Lord, thank You that Your favor is making a way." If you work in real estate, keep declaring, "Lord, thank You that Your favor is shining down on my properties and causing them to sell." God wants to help you in the everyday things of life, not just the big things.

One time Victoria and I were taking our children to the zoo. It was about ten o'clock in the morning. We didn't think anybody would be there. But when we arrived, the place was packed. We didn't realize it was spring break and all the children were out of school. The parking lot was so backed up with traffic. People were everywhere. We drove around and around the parking area, up and down, back and forth, and couldn't find any place to park. Just as we were about to leave, I did what I'm asking you to do. Under my breath I said, "Lord, thank You for Your favor. Thank You for helping us find a parking spot so we can have fun with our children."

This is not a magic formula. I was simply acknowledging God. The Scripture says, "When you acknowledge God, He will crown your efforts with success." A couple minutes later, just as if it was perfectly on cue, as I was driving around a car backed out. We were able to pull in. My first words were, "Lord, thank You for Your favor."

When something good happens, recognize that it's the favor of God and then learn to thank Him for it. At the office, all of a sudden you have a good idea. It comes out of nowhere. "Lord, thank You for Your favor." At the mall you find what you want on sale. At lunch you bump into somebody you've been wanting to meet. Those aren't lucky breaks. Those aren't coincidences. That's the favor of God. If you will recognize it and thank God for it, you'll see more of His favor.

I was at the mall a few years ago with Victoria. She had a couple things she wanted to buy, so I went up to the counter to pay. I was just minding my own business. I said hello to the lady and smiled, no big deal. She said, "This blouse goes on sale this weekend. I'll go ahead and give you the sale price today." After I thanked her, under my breath I said, "Lord, thank You for Your favor."

She looked at the other shirt. At the very bottom there was a little place where the fabric was messed up. You could barely even see it, very minor. She said, "That's not right. Let me see what I can do." She went to talk to her manager, then came back and said, "If it's okay with you, we'll mark this down to half price." I said, "I guess it will be okay." She didn't have to do that. I wouldn't have known any difference. That was the favor of God causing people to be good to me. I walked out of there saying, "Lord, thank You for Your favor. I recognize Your goodness in my life." When you live favor-minded, God will cause good breaks to chase you down. He will cause people to go out of their way to do you favors.

David understood this principle. He said, "Surely goodness and mercy will follow me all the days of my life." He was saying, "Favor follows me everywhere I go." David knew he had an advantage. He knew God would assist him, that he could expect preferential treatment. He was living with a favor mind-set.

> *He was living with a favor mind-set.*

The truth is, something is going to follow you throughout life. If you go around thinking, *I never get any good breaks. Nothing good ever happens to me*, then defeat, lack, and mediocrity will follow you around. You need to switch over into this favor mind-set and have the attitude, *God's favor is giving me advantages. God's favor is causing me to stand out. God's favor is bringing victory into my life.* When you live like that, good breaks will chase you down. Favor, increase, and promotion will follow you.

Favor Shines on You

What would happen if we would get up each day and pray this simple prayer from Genesis 12:2? "God, thank You today for an abundant increase of Your favor. Lord, thank You in advance for assisting me, for providing me with advantages, for causing me to have preferential treatment." That's how you will step into the fullness of your destiny.

I talked to a gentleman who was in town for a job interview. It was a very important position. Executives were flying in from around the country to interview for this job. He really wanted it, but he told me that he wasn't the most qualified, didn't have the most experience, on and on, all the reasons why he shouldn't get it. I told him what I'm telling you. Every day you need to speak favor over that situation. "Father, thank You that Your favor is causing me to stand out. Lord, thank You that Your favor is shining down on me, causing them to want to hire me." I saw him several months later, and he was beaming from ear to ear. I knew he had gotten the position. He said, "Joel, it was the strangest thing. When the executives called me in to give me the good news, they were scratching their heads. They said, 'We don't really know why we're hiring you. You're not the most qualified. You don't have the best résumé. There's just something about you that we like. There's something...we can't put our finger on it, but it causes you to stand out.'"

That's what it says in the book of Numbers. "God will make His face shine down upon you and give you His favor." When you live favor-minded, it's like a bright light shining down on you.

> *When you live favor-minded, it's like a bright light shining down on you.*

It will cause you to go places you could not go on your own. Other people may have more talent, more experience, more education, but the favor of God will cause you to stand out. Every day you need to imagine that you're not only wearing a crown of favor but that God's light is shining down on you. You are glowing with God's goodness. You are radiating with God's favor. Now get up every morning expecting it and declaring it—not because of who you are but because of Whose you are. Remember, you've been born into the right family. You've come from a royal bloodline.

If you develop this habit of living favor-minded, I believe and declare that God is going to assist you, provide you with advantages, and cause you to have preferential treatment. You need to get ready. You're going to see an abundant increase of favor.

CHAPTER SIXTEEN

Heavy with Favor

In the previous chapter, I noted that the psalmist said, "God's favor surrounds us like a shield," which means everywhere you go you have an advantage, a divine empowerment, opening up the right doors, causing things to fall into place. But the prophet Isaiah took it a step further. He said, "Arise and shine, for the glory of the Lord is upon you." That word *glory* in the original language implies God's favor is heavy upon you. There is an emphasis on the weight. Isaiah was saying, "You didn't just get a little favor, enough to get by, to scrape through life." No, when it comes to favor, you're not a lightweight. You are heavy with favor. You are weighted down with God's goodness.

It's one thing to know you have favor. That's important, but when you realize you are heavy with favor, it takes on a whole new meaning. You won't go around intimidated or insecure. You'll put your shoulders back, hold your head high. When you know you have heavy favor, you'll pray bold prayers. You'll believe for the extraordinary. You'll expect doors to open for you that may not open for somebody else. You'll expect to pay off your house, to break the addiction, to see your children be mighty in the land. When you know you're heavy with favor, you'll arise, and that's when God will cause you to shine. You'll step into a new level of your destiny.

Maybe you're heavy with worry, heavy with discouragement, weighted down with problems, disappointments, sickness, and lack. You need to get ready. Things are about to turn in your favor. Instead of being heavy with burdens, you're going to be heavy with good breaks, heavy with divine health, heavy with opportunity, heavy with joy.

I remember back in the '60s that when something good happened, hippies would say, "Heavy, man. Heavy." That's what you're going to be saying. Out of nowhere a good break comes. "Heavy, man. Heavy." The medical report didn't look good, but your health suddenly turns around. "Heavy, man. Heavy." In your finances you receive an explosive blessing—a bonus, a raise, an inheritance—and you pay off your house, you come out of debt into overflow. "Heavy, man. Heavy." Now shake off the doubt. Shake off the discouragement. Have a new perspective. You

> *You didn't get average favor, ordinary favor, just enough favor. You are heavy with favor.*

didn't get average favor, ordinary favor, just enough favor. You are heavy with favor. When you understand this, it will change your outlook. You'll have a boldness, a confidence to ask big, to believe big, to expect God's favor in a new way.

Dare to Do as Joshua Did

In the Scripture, Joshua and his men were out fighting a battle. It was getting late in the day, and he knew he wasn't going to be able to finish the enemy off because he was running out of daylight. He could have thought, *Too bad for me. I've run out of time.* No, Joshua understood this principle. He knew he was heavy with favor. He looked up and said, "Sun, stand still." The Scripture says the Sun stopped and didn't go down until he completed his task. When you know you're heavy with favor, instead of thinking, *Oh, man, this problem is never going to be resolved*, you'll do as Joshua did and say, "God, I may not see a way but I know You have a way." "The medical report doesn't look good, but God, I know You have the final say. Healing is coming my way." "It doesn't look as though I'll ever get out of debt, but God, I know You own it all. Increase is coming my way." Or maybe, "I've had this addiction for so long, but I know this is my time. Freedom is coming my way."

I wonder how much further we would go, how many dreams we would see come to pass, if we really believed we are heavy with favor. Are you praying these bold prayers, expecting God to show out in your life? Would you dare do as Joshua did and ask God to do something out of the ordinary, to bring your dreams to pass even though they look so far out, as though they're not practical? It may not be for an average person, but the good news is, you're not

average. You have heavy favor. This is your time to arise
and shine. God is about to make you stand out. He is about
to take you somewhere you've never been. Now all through
the day get in agreement with God and say, "Lord, thank
You that I'm heavy with favor. You are shining down on
me, showing me something that I've never seen."

A few years ago a friend of mine sold his house. He and
his family needed another place to live. They had looked at
house after house and couldn't find what they wanted. One
evening they were out walking through their neighborhood
when he saw this one house that he had always liked. He
liked the look, the layout, the location, everything about it.
The owners had lived there for over thirty years, but something inside my friend said, "Go and ask them if they want
to sell it." He thought, *I can't do that. That would be odd,
a stranger knocking on their door.* He's a very quiet, reserved
man, but he couldn't get away from that feeling. He finally
got his nerve up, went and knocked on the door and asked
the man if he was interested in selling the house.

The man said, "No, we're planning on living here for
many more years."

My friend handed him his business card and said, "Well,
if you ever change your mind, please let me know."

Five days later, the man called back and said, "We've
had a change of heart. We'd like to sell you the house."

Now my friend lives in the beautiful house he always
wanted. What is that? Heavy favor. To knock on somebody's door and then find them willing to move out of

their house—only God can make that happen. Don't come knocking on my door now. But when you know that you have heavy favor, you'll have this boldness, this confidence, to ask big, to believe big. That's when God will show out in your life. But too often we think, *Oh, this isn't going to happen for me. I never get any good breaks. I'll never live in a nice place. I'll never break this addiction, never get healthy again.* Get rid of that defeated mentality. Have this new perspective: You are heavy with favor. This is your time to rise higher, to come into overflow, to see those dreams come to pass. Now be bold. Dare to take some steps of faith. Dare to believe. God has already given you everything you need. Thoughts will try to talk you out of it, tell you why it's not going to happen. You have to talk back to yourself the right way. "Lord, I want to thank You that You are shining down on me. This is my due season. Dreams are coming to pass. These problems are turning around. Lord, I believe I'm heavy with favor." When you live with this expectancy, you'll see God do things that are out of the ordinary.

> *This is your time to rise higher, to come into overflow, to see those dreams come to pass.*

You Have Because You Ask

In 2003, we had our groundbreaking services planned for the renovation of our building, the former Compaq Center.

We were going to have one weekend where everyone could see it, then it was going to take a year and a half to finish the construction. We had this big weekend all lined up when we got word that the highway department was going to close the freeway down a few hours before our services. Very few people would have been able to come, but we couldn't change our plans. We had already advertised, already rented all the equipment. We could have thought, *We sure chose the wrong weekend for the groundbreaking.* But the Scripture says, "You have not because you ask not." How many things are we not seeing God do, not because He won't do it but because we're not asking? We called the highway department and asked if they would change their plans for our services. They kind of laughed and said, "We're sorry, but we don't do that. This construction has been planned for years." But when you know you're heavy with favor, you don't give up just because you are rejected one time. You go back and ask again.

We got in touch with the main person in the highway department. He called back a few days later and said, "We've never done this before, but we're going to make an exception for you and wait to close the freeway until after your services are over." If you're going to see the fullness of your destiny, you have to have this boldness to ask big, to believe big, to expect things to happen for you that may not happen for somebody else. Not arrogantly, but in humility, dare to believe. There is something on you that causes people to want to be good to you. Something that causes you to get breaks that you don't deserve. Something that causes problems that looked permanent to suddenly turn around. What is it? It's heavy favor.

I know a couple whose daughter was three years old when something fell on two of her fingers and cut the very tips off them. They rushed her to the emergency room. The surgeon eventually told the father, "I'm sorry, but there's nothing I'm going to be able to do to restore your daughter's two fingers. She will never have fingernails on those fingers. Plus, they will always be a little bit shorter. The bone is missing." The surgeon said that all he could do was a skin graft and try to smooth it over.

This father was respectful, but he knew he had heavy favor. He said, "Doctor, I believe God can restore my little girl's fingers and make them normal again."

The doctor didn't understand much about faith. He looked at the man and said, "Well, that's fine, sir. You can believe whatever you want. I'm just telling you the bone is missing. Those fingers will never be the right length."

When the man's wife came in, the doctor took her over to the side and said, "Your husband is in shock. He won't accept the fact that the tips of your daughter's fingers have been cut off."

The little girl had the skin graft, and six weeks later they brought her back for her checkup. When the doctor removed the bandages, his first words were, "Oh my God!"

This father was alarmed and said, "What's wrong?"

The doctor said, "Look. The fingernails have grown back, and it looks like the two fingers are the exact right length."

That was years ago. Those two fingers are still perfectly normal. When you believe you are heavy with favor, you will see things happen that look impossible. You may be in a situation right now where all the odds are against you. The experts say it's not going to happen. You won't get well, won't qualify for the house loan, won't see the dream come to pass. But what they are not taking into account is the favor on your life. If it was average favor, you may be stuck. It may not happen. But the difference is, you don't have average favor. You have heavy favor. God is about to show out in your life. He is about to turn some things around. You're going to look up and say as this couple did, "That was heavy favor. That was the goodness of God." Dare to believe big. Dare to pray big. God wants to do something that you've never seen, something out of the ordinary.

More Than You Can Ask or Think

Doctor Todd Price is a friend of mine. He attends Lakewood. He has a successful infectious disease practice in Houston. He also does medical mission work all over the world. Several years back, when he was first getting started with his medical outreaches, he had a dream to take shoes to needy children in Africa. He said that because the children didn't wear shoes, 80 percent of them had parasites, and it was ruining their health. But Dr. Price is just one person, with a busy medical practice. How could he make much of a difference? Because he understands that he has heavy favor, he had the boldness to ask the big medical companies and suppliers to help him out. His goal was to take shoes to all the children in a particular village where he was working at that time—three thousand kids.

A shoe company here in the States heard what he was doing, called him, and asked, "How many pairs of shoes do you need?"

He said, "Three thousand pairs."

They said, "We have a few more than three thousand. How about we give you one hundred thousand pairs of children shoes?"

That's heavy favor. That's the way God is. When you dream big, believe big, expect big, God will supersize what you're dreaming about. And some of you—what you're praying for is way too small. What you're hoping you can accomplish is not near what God has in mind. You need to get ready. God is about to supersize it. You're going to see this heavy favor.

> *When you dream big, believe big, expect big, God will supersize what you're dreaming about.*

The Scripture says, "You haven't seen, heard, or imagined the amazing things God has in store for those who love the Lord." That's you.

I've seen this happen in my own life again and again.

What I thought would be so great, what I was hoping to accomplish, was nothing compared to what God had in mind. In my early twenties, when I walked into the jewelry store and met Victoria for the first time, she was one of those things I had not seen, heard, or imagined. God supersized what I was dreaming about. It took heavy favor to get her, let me tell you. It takes heavy favor to keep her.

Fifteen years ago, when I wrote my first book, *Your Best Life Now*, I thought, *Wouldn't that be amazing if it made the* New York Times *Bestseller list?* I would have been thrilled if it would have made it just for one week. That book was on the list for over one hundred weeks in a row. God supersized what I was dreaming about.

When we moved into what had been the Compaq Center, we signed a sixty-year lease with the City of Houston. We always knew we wanted to purchase it, but the lease was the best option at the time. This facility is worth several hundred million dollars. In 2010, the city contacted us and asked if we were interested in purchasing it. We told them we were, but, of course, it all depended on the price. They did all their studies. After their evaluations, they called us back and said, "We'll sell it to you, not for one hundred million, not fifty million, not twenty-five million. We'll sell it to you for seven and a half million dollars." That's heavy favor. That's more than we could ask or think.

The apostle Paul said, "In the ages to come we would see the surpassing greatness of God's favor." We are living in the day Paul talked about, when we will see far-and-beyond favor. If you get your hopes up, start expecting it, praying bold prayers, believing for the extraordinary, when you arise, God will cause you to shine. He will show up and supersize what you're dreaming about.

A couple who attend Lakewood have a daughter who had a heart defect. She had to have several very extensive surgeries. Today, the young lady is perfectly healthy. But those surgeries were not fully covered by their insurance. Their part of the hospital bill was over $400,000. The mother is a schoolteacher, and the father is a police officer. In the natural, it looked as though they would be paying on that debt for a long, long time. But they didn't get discouraged. They didn't start complaining. They knew they had heavy favor. They dared to pray these bold prayers. They said, "God, we don't see how we can get out of debt, but we know You own it all. One touch of Your favor can turn it around."

One day, out of the blue, the hospital called and said, "We've never done this before, but we've decided to not only forgive your debt, but we're going to pay you back for the two years of payments you've already made." They were just hoping to be debt free, but God supersized what they were dreaming about. He will do it for you.

Always More Powerful

In Second Kings 6, an enemy army was trying to overtake the Israelites, but every time they made a move the Israelites already knew where they were going. The enemy king was so frustrated because he thought one of his men was a spy. He called them together and said, "Who's the traitor? Who's leaking this inside information?"

A captain spoke up and said, "King, it's none of us. There's a prophet in Israel named Elisha. What you whisper to us in secret he announces publicly to the Israelites."

The king was furious and said, "We're going to get Elisha." So one night he sent a great army with many horses and chariots to surround Elisha's house. Notice what happens when you're heavy with favor. This king was trying to capture one man. You would think he might send a dozen people to get Elisha, but he sent thousands of troops, horses, and chariots, all to capture one man who was heavy with favor.

Elisha's assistant got up early in the morning and saw all the enemy forces surrounding the house. When he told Elisha in a panic about it, Elisha said, "Don't worry. We may be outnumbered, but I know a secret. I'm heavy with favor. They may have more weapons, more equipment, more talent. But I have something more powerful than all of that—the favor of God."

Elisha knew how to pray these bold prayers. He had seen God open blind eyes. Now he prayed for just the opposite. He said, "God, let them become blind so they don't recognize me."

Blinded, the enemy leaders came and knocked on the door and said, "We're looking for Elisha."

He said, "Elisha? You're in the wrong city. You need to go to Samaria."

They said, "Thank you, sir, for your help."

He said, "Let me help you some more. I'll lead you to the man you seek."

Elisha ended up leading the enemy army right into the hands of the Israelites. Once they were surrounded and captured, Elisha prayed again and their eyes were opened. They realized it was Elisha the whole time. When you know you're heavy with favor, you'll see God do amazing things. He will protect you from your enemies. He will guide you. He will even make you invisible to your enemies. Now don't you dare go around weak, afraid, and intimidated. You are so powerful. You are full of the anointing. You are heavy with favor. When the enemy looks at you, just as with Elisha, he thinks, *I have to send a whole army to try to stop him*. He may do his best, but his best will never be enough. When you're heavy with favor, you cannot be defeated.

> *When you know you're heavy with favor, you'll see God do amazing things.*

Nothing Too Hard

When my father was a young minister back in the 1950s, he would travel from town to town, speaking in small churches and conventions. He carried his sound equipment in the trunk of his car. One evening he arrived at an auditorium a couple hours early to get everything set up. Several hundred people were expected that night. It was a big deal for my father. He wanted it to all go perfect. But in the midst of the excitement he accidentally locked his keys in the trunk of his car. He couldn't get the sound equipment out. He and some other people started working on the trunk, shaking it, jiggling it, using a coat hanger to try to get it open. No success. It looked as though his big evening was ruined.

Just when he was about to give up he realized he hadn't prayed. One thing I can tell you about my father is that he knew how to pray these bold prayers. He wasn't ashamed to pray about anything. When I was growing up, he would pray over the lawnmower, over the dishwasher, over anything that wouldn't work.

My father told all the people standing there that he was going to pray and ask God to help open the trunk. They looked at him so strange. That seemed so far out. They were thinking, *You can't pray for a trunk to be opened.* But my father did. He said, "God, I know there is nothing too hard for You. Lord, I need this sound equipment for my meeting tonight. So I'm asking You to somehow, some way, help me to get it open."

While he was praying, the other people were laughing, mocking, making fun under their breath. When he finished praying, he went over to the trunk and began to shake it and jiggle it even harder than ever, but it still wouldn't open. Finally, he turned and walked away. When he got about ten feet from the car, they all heard a *click*. They looked back, and all on its own, in slow motion, that trunk began to slowly open up. Just like it was saying, "Hallelujah!" Those other people nearly passed out. My father had one of the best meetings of his life that night. He had their attention.

You may not need a trunk to open, but perhaps the doctors have told you that it doesn't look good. Why don't you arise and say, "God, I believe I'm heavy with favor and that You can do what medicine cannot do." Or perhaps your child is off course. You're struggling in your finances. Your dream looks impossible. Have you ever asked God to turn it around? Have you ever said, "God, I know nothing is too hard for You. You have the final say. You can get me to where I'm supposed to be." When you have this heavy favor, you'll have a boldness to believe for the fullness of your destiny.

Believing Is the Key

Luke 1 speaks about an ordinary teenaged girl named Mary. She didn't come from an influential family. Her parents weren't wealthy or famous. They were poor. In the natural, there was nothing special about Mary, nothing that made her stand out. But one day an angel appeared to her and said, "Hello, Mary, you highly favored woman."

I'm sure at first she looked around and thought, *You have the wrong girl. I'm not highly favored. I'm just average.*

It's easy to talk yourself out of what God has said about you. But if an angel were to appear to you today, he would say the same thing. "Hello, James, you highly favored man."

"Hello, Marie, you highly favored woman." "Hello, Lakewood, you highly favored people." The angel went on to tell Mary that she was going to have a baby without knowing a man. Sometimes God will put things in your heart that seem very unlikely. That's why the angel started off the conversation by reminding her that she was heavy with favor. When you face impossible situations, you have to remind yourself that like Mary, you too are heavy with God's favor.

Later, Mary's older cousin Elizabeth said to her, "You are blessed because you believed the Lord will do what He said." Notice that believing is the key. In

> *Believing is the key.*

other words, even though the angel said she was heavy with favor, if she had not believed it, she would have never seen this favor.

God is saying to you today, "This is your due season. Dreams are coming to pass. Problems are turning around. You're about to rise to a new level." You can either let circumstances talk you out of it or you can do as Mary did and say, "God, I agree. I believe I'm heavy with favor." When you arise, God will cause you to shine.

What I'm saying is, you're not a lightweight. You didn't get average favor, ordinary favor. You are heavy with favor. Dare to believe big. Pray these bold prayers. Expect God to do the extraordinary. If you do this, I believe and declare you haven't seen, heard, or imagined what's coming your way. God is about to show out in your life. Get ready for breakthroughs, for promotion, for healing, for a new level of your destiny.

ACKNOWLEDGMENTS

In this book I offer many stories shared with me by friends, members of our congregation, and people I've met around the world. I appreciate and acknowledge their contributions and support. Some of those mentioned in the book are people I have not met personally, and in a few cases, we've changed the names to protect the privacy of individuals. I give honor to all those to whom honor is due. As the son of a church leader and a pastor myself, I've listened to countless sermons and presentations, so in some cases I can't remember the exact source of a story.

I am indebted to the amazing staff of Lakewood Church, the wonderful members of Lakewood who share their stories with me, and those around the world who generously support our ministry and make it possible to bring hope to a world in need. I am grateful to all those who follow our services on television, the Internet, SiriusXM, and through the podcasts. You are all part of our Lakewood family.

I offer special thanks also to all the pastors across the country who are members of our Champions Network.

Once again, I am grateful for a wonderful team of professionals who helped me put this book together for you. Leading them is my FaithWords/Hachette publisher, Rolf Zettersten, along with team members Patsy Jones, Billy Clark, and Karin Mathis. I truly appreciate the editorial contributions of wordsmith Lance Wubbels.

I am grateful also to my literary agents Jan Miller Rich and Shannon Marven at Dupree Miller & Associates.

And last but not least, thanks to my wife, Victoria, and our children, Jonathan and Alexandra, who are my sources of daily inspiration, as well as our closest family members, who serve as day-to-day leaders of our ministry, including my mother, Dodie; my brother, Paul, and his wife, Jennifer; my sister Lisa and her husband, Kevin; and my brother-in-law Don and his wife, Jackelyn.

We Want to Hear from You!

Each week, I close our international television broadcast by giving the audience an opportunity to make Jesus the Lord of their lives. I'd like to extend that same opportunity to you.

Are you at peace with God? A void exists in every person's heart that only God can fill. I'm not talking about joining a church or finding religion. I'm talking about finding life and peace and happiness. Would you pray with me today? Just say, "Lord Jesus, I repent of my sins. I ask You to come into my heart. I make You my Lord and Savior."

Friend, if you prayed that simple prayer, I believe you have been "born again." I encourage you to attend a good Bible-based church and keep God in first place in your life. For free information on how you can grow stronger in your spiritual life, please feel free to contact us.

Victoria and I love you, and we'll be praying for you. We're believing for God's best for you, that you will see your dreams come to pass. We'd love to hear from you!

To contact us, write to:

Joel and Victoria Osteen
P.O. Box 4600
Houston, TX 77210

Or you can reach us online at www.joelosteen.com.